# ADVANCE PRAISE FOR *YOU SAY, I SAY*

"*You Say, I Say* is a joy and privilege to read. Two college friends, decades later, exchange letters about what matters most: family, friendship, the history of literature from Homer to Kafka. I am deeply grateful to be able to follow the exchange—to learn from them as they learn from each other. The book is a testament to how literature—and the questions literature allows us to ask—sustains us."—Josh Kotin, Associate Professor of English and Director of the Graduate Program, Princeton University

"The missives, originally sent as e-mails, have a conversational style and reflect a delightful blend of jargon-free literary banter, featuring the learned insights of two people who share a profound love of the written word. . . . In each of the book's 33 letters, readers will experience a poignant and accessible ode to reading and writing. A touching anthology of correspondence between two friends that's also a love letter to literature."—*Kirkus Reviews*

"Incisive, edifying letters between friends exploring life, lit, and more. . . . Waxler writes movingly of literature's magic and origins, and his and Beckman's letters show the depth and passion that words can inspire, even if ultimate meaning remains elusive. As Waxler notes, in his scrupulous prose, 'Through literature, we find the questions we need, if not the answers we want.' "—*Publishers Weekly BookLife*

"Bob Waxler's and David Beckman's new book proves that the quest for meaning does not end with graduation. Their conversation makes a refreshing book and proves how well curiosity can age."—James Marlow, author of *Charles Dickens: Uses of Time*

"The authors' reflections, threaded into the fabric of memoir, create a narrative path that will draw readers in to contemplate the significance of friendship, of ideas, of language, and of the literary imagination."—Martha C. Pennington, Visiting Professor of English Language and Applied Linguistics at the University of Reading (UK)

"The writing is superb . . . which comes as no surprise. David Beckman and I worked together for years in the magazine business, and his writing was always thoughtful and wonderfully creative. Now he and Bob Waxler have combined to create a grand example of their prodigious skill."—Jim Hayes, Publisher Emeritus, *Discover* and *Fortune* magazines

"In their heartfelt and engaging literary conversation, *You Say, I Say,* Waxler and Beckman find meaning in quiet corners while chaos reigns around us. They unearth gems of philosophy, battle their private demons, and share their love of reading and writing, giving us hope that literature, language, and friendship can indeed keep us alive."—Jean Trounstine, professor, activist, co-founder of the women's branch of Changing Lives Through Literature, and author of eight books, including *Sounds Like Trouble to Me* (Running Wild Pub, 2026)

"Writing letters, some say, is a dead art. In these letters between two old college friends who happen to be writers, we are invited to experience conversations both personal and academic. The joy of rediscovering each other after many years is felt, while their letters, often raising questions that needn't be fully answered yet give us pause to contemplate the possibilities anyway, are far-ranging. Is it necessary to 'rebel against silence' in order to write? What if language says more than it knows? Was Wordsworth a rabbi of sorts? Within these pages are contemplations from the Bible to Homer to Mary Oliver and Marge Piercy. In the process of sharing their questions and thoughts, Beckman and Waxler learn from each other. Why, for instance, did Blake 'downplay memory?' It is a gift that the memories these friends shared brought them together again to write to each other and, it turns out, to us. Long live the writing of letters."—Katherine Hastings, Poet Laureate Emerita of Sonoma County

"A German friend once said to me, 'American men are typically wary of serious conversation.' I agreed. But now I have a strong counter-example. *You Say, I Say* offers an engaging and intense conversation where we participate in an unfolding process of resisting conclusions so that we can join two fine minds exploring their capacities to deepen the activity of reflection. That activity here means examining presuppositions, constantly questioning what could serve as answers were there not the need to respond to another mind absorbed by the same issues. Ultimately this ideal of conversation is grounded in an elaborate contrast between the Hebrew *davar* and the Greek *logos*. The authors emphasize how the Hebrew term refers to the density of affective life embodied in linguistic activity, while the Greek lays the groundwork for the idealization of analytic reasoning. How the authors enact this distinction makes me want to correct the book's title to add 'We think together.' They do so exceptionally well on the topics like silence and all the ramifications of cultivating *davar*."—Charles Altieri, Professor Emeritus and Rachael Anderson Stageberg Chair Emeritus, University of California at Berkeley

# You Say, I Say

## STAYING ALIVE WITH LITERATURE, LANGUAGE, AND FRIENDSHIP

## Robert Waxler &
## David Beckman

 **Rivertowns**
**BOOKS**
IRVINGTON, NEW YORK

Hardcover edition ISBN-13: 978-1-953943-61-3
Paperback edition ISBN-13: 978-1-953943-62-0
Ebook edition ISBN-13: 978-1-953943-63-7

LCCN Imprint Name: Rivertowns Books
Library of Congress Control Number: 2025938809

Rivertowns Books are available from all bookshops, other stores that carry books, online retailers, and directly from the publisher. Visit our website at www.rivertownsbooks.com. Retailer and consumer orders, inquiries about discounts for bulk purchases, and other correspondence may be addressed to:

Rivertowns Books
240 Locust Lane
Irvington NY 10533
Email: info@rivertownsbooks.com

To Linda, Jeremy, and Jonathan—
for now and forever

ROBERT WAXLER

For Sharon, designer and art director, marketer and charity
volunteer, my wife and best friend

DAVID BECKMAN

# Contents

# Introduction

We met as college freshman a near-lifetime ago, two 18-year-olds at Brown University in September, 1962, aware and unaware. Aware of possibility and newfound freedom, and a gestating creativity with language; unaware of so much else, including the furrows that time would slowly etch into our faces.

Over the next few undergraduate years, we became part of a circle of friends, seemingly close, but not, in hindsight, close enough to weather intact the eventual triad of time, adulthood, and distance.

For the two of us, our bond culminated in a poetry chapbook, *Echo Aonides,* that we published our senior year—our debut as aspiring poets. We were particularly proud of the title—sufficiently obscure, implying our descent from things Aonian, including Mount Helicon, home of the Muses, whom Ovid called the Aonides. Our little book caused a small buzz on campus and in our heads. We were interviewed; we had success in a nutshell.

Then we graduated, walking through the Van Wickle Gates and down Benefit Street into the wider world. Bob made his way to a PhD and a college professorship in literature, David to a career in commercial writing with sidelines in acting, poetry, and playwriting. We married and prospered, Bob teaching at UMass Dartmouth, David writing advertising in New York City. Bob and his wife Linda had children; David and his wife Sharon chose not to. Over time, we lost touch with one another, and lost something else—what had been an important early friendship.

In 2014, Bob posted an article in the *Brown Alumni Magazine* (with his email address), and David reached out immediately. An avid correspondence followed, and we both rediscovered what had bonded us initially—our love of language and literature and our attachment to the written word as a springboard to self-exploration, all now deepened immeasurably by the act of living.

We and our wives met up in New York and, later, in Providence, and in 2020, in Dartmouth, Massachusetts, where Bob showed David his stack of handwritten notebooks with thoughts and commentaries on the dozen and more writers, poets, and thinkers in which he had immersed himself for years.

The next step came naturally—an ongoing, coast-to-coast email correspondence with two goals: to renew and deepen our friendship, and to explore together some of what we'd learned about life and language in the years since Brown. It grew into a written dialogue ranging across space, time, experience, memory, reading, and reflection. Gradually, it revealed a shared search for what literature demands: patience, belief, embracing of the self even while letting it go. And for what literature gives back: breath, wonder, connection, and celebration of that elusive thing called spirit.

The flow of emails began on May 21, 2021, and ended on October 2, 2024. Toward the middle of 2024 it occurred to us that they could constitute a book. And so they do now.

What were emails we now call "letters," perhaps from an impulse to give them heft. Taken together, they form a sort of joint memoir, capturing, we hope, the spontaneity of conversation, with loose-form excursions across memory, time, language, and literature.

*You Say, I Say* is a gift to ourselves, to each other, and to the very different worlds we've known, struggled with, made peace with, and loved. But more, we hope it may provide some moments of insight and enjoyment for readers who share our appreciation for the beauty and power of the Word. And our love of friendship.

Robert Waxler, Dartmouth, Massachusetts
David Beckman, Santa Rosa, California

# 1. Settling In

David,

I'm glad you are settling in. I appreciate your willingness to catch up on our old friendship, and take the plunge back into what animated us decades ago—poetry, literature, writing as gateways to who we are. It might be rewarding and interesting if you begin by writing about your own work and thinking related to language and literature.

For my part, I might draw on some of the topics I have scattered throughout my notebooks these days—a variety of wandering thoughts that capture questions I'm interested in. And as a friend, though, let me tell you this from the start: I am more interested in the questions that the path of such wandering leads to than the home that might provide final answers to those questions. It is a kind of quest that I envision, an exploration of language and literature in relation to the ineffable, in relation to the ethical imagination, in relation to silence and voice, in relation to representation, in relation to "nothingness," in relation to prayer, and in relation to revelation and to reason.

So any direction mentioned here, or not mentioned yet, is certainly welcome.

Bob

# 2. Plunging In

Bob,

What a pleasure, and challenge, not only to reconnect, but to commit to this project, if *project* is not too bloodless a term. Perhaps, rather, *journey*, presenting the chance to set the clock back decades while also urging it forward. This is not to deprecate the present, the place that we writers must fully inhabit, and that I look forward to occupying with you again. Yes, *again*, because we were once here before as young college friends. And now, with luck, we'll be friends again, exploring a special relationship built around our mutual love of language and literature.

As I have hinted at, if not fully unpacked, my long post-college writing life had two tracks—one as commercial writer for hire, one as poet and playwright. Together they shaped my relationship with myself, with the world, and—our primary topic here—with words.

In professional writing, I couldn't afford dry spells, and so had to force creativity. With poetry, the opposite was true: To force a poem into being is to mar its nature before it's born. Yet a poet must write poems! Failing to do so is the same as failing to produce an assignment as a commercial writer. In both cases, the winner is silence.

Do you find in beginning any piece of writing, poetry or prose, that writing that first line is not so much breaking silence as rebelling against it?

It's true for me. Silence is, ultimately, a tyrant, enforcing its own mysterious, nihilistic need (one bereft of language). To challenge its power is rebellion, and so both risk-taking and life-giving.

Having thus broken the ice here (or, indeed, the silence) I'll be so bold as to offer an example. After Sharon and I ended our visit with you and Linda in Dartmouth last week, we drove to Copake, New York, to spend a few days with my friend Marty Butensky. Sitting beside his swimming pool, I was very willing to enjoy an hour of quiet pleasure. Yet, out of the silence, these nine words came to me:

And so I return to music by the pool

Having no laptop handy, I quickly fetched a pad and pen, and wrote them down. This was my small act of rebellion, pitting myself against silence. I was balanced on the edge of language, awaiting an outcome.

Silence was offended and shocked, but also back on its heels, and so a second and third line came easier:

and watch the water's blue ripples
kiss and kiss again the pool's concrete walkway.

Good poetry? I didn't care, because I had an agenda . . . language yanking a new reality, one that didn't exist before, from the grip of silence. As long as I could keep writing, I had the upper hand.

Of course, I well knew that even if I finished the poem, silence would return, exerting its force until I rebelled again.

What strikes me is that in launching our journey, this written conversation, we're breaking silence ourselves (that decades-long silence between us), rebelling against its pull toward dominance. Of course, our language here is prose, which raises the interesting question of how any particular writing form is less or more aggressive toward silence than any other. Remembering our love of sixties ballads, most of all those by Bob Dylan, I'll ask if a song is the bravest foray, in which melody and lyric, fragile in a sense, risk all? Or is it the opposite, as the voice given over to singing empowers the spirit, making it indominable?

What about purely oral poetry? Maybe too rare in our culture unless you include hearing (rather than reading) a Shakespeare play, or exceptional song lyrics. With this, doesn't Dylan loom large again with his winning the Nobel Prize for Literature? Was his work as much oral poetry, as it was song? The Nobel committee seemed to think so.

Finally, prose, our current shared form and, after all, the root of *prosaic*, the latter carrying a note of disparagement. Is it that we speak routinely in prose, and, in doing so, fail to experience ourselves as breaking silence in any courageous sense? Indeed, the spoken word can be mundane or worse—cowardly, even violent. At the same time, as self-revelation, testimony, confession, or declaration of love, it can be deeply affecting and honest. And so as powerful a pushing away of silence as any poem or song.

I hope that what we're doing is charged enough, urgent enough in both our minds, that it is on the level of that kind of prose, or, indeed, poetry.

Bob, in winding down this first e-letter to you, I am very aware of your working life as literature professor, and your specialty, William Blake. His work has always struck me as a bold foray against silence. Why with him more than, say, Keats, or Shelley? I'd welcome your views on this.

But I'm led to his "fearful symmetry." Am I right that in his poem "The Tyger," that he saw both the tiger's destructive potential and its beauty seamlessly joined? And had resolved, in language, the awful duality of destruction and creation?

Where do language and silence come into this? Of course, one can't pose this question without going to the critic George Steiner and his book (what else?) *Language and Silence* where, on the theme of the holocaust, he famously wrote that "Auschwitz lies outside of speech, as it lies outside reason."

For Steiner, Auschwitz was unspeakable, a despoiler of language. Ultimately, if a thing is not to be spoken of, perhaps what's key is the motivation for silence. The survivors of Auschwitz may have initially been unable to speak of it because of trauma, shame, pain, or loss. Yet, in fact, many have.

And the perpetrators, the Nazi commanders at Nuremberg, sitting stone-faced and silent, what of them? Does their silence

In the face of atrocity, silence is a violation of humanity

6

violate humanity all over again, allowing the loss of memory to take root and prevail?

In this context, can the horrific and the beautiful exist side by side? If a tiger attacks, one swipe of its paw can kill us, clawing the flesh from our chest and leaving only the bared ribs housing the heart in its death seizure. Conversely, the tiger can step back, pose unwittingly, show us his utter beauty of line, color, and balance, such that we (with Blake) think, Yes, God resides there, in that tiger, as what in His creation could be more beautiful? Perhaps there is a point at which language fails, leaving silence as the most eloquent response.

May I return to my poem by the pool, and continue it?

> The sun passes overhead, eyes the pool,
> extends down transparent fingers to touch
> (not kiss!) the ripples as if it owns them
> at least till nightfall.

David

# 3. A Pathway Emerges

David,

Y our letter suggests an important pathway to begin our walk through language and literature. You've got me thinking about the Holocaust (as reflected in the writings of George Steiner and Theodor Adorno, for example), and, by contrast, my favorite poets, the English Romantics. My recent reading from the biblical texts—especially the creation story and the beginning of the Gospel of John—also strike me as relevant here. I'm also eager to start a dialogue with you about your poem by the pool.

I want to alert you again, though: I am, and am not, the same person who met you when we were undergraduates in those remarkable days at Brown, days when we would look forward to late-night discussion about literature and philosophy (and some refreshing cold beer). I had a plan in those days which I taped to my bedroom wall: "Write a book of poems (or a novel) before your 25th birthday—or kill yourself." On the dormitory bulletin board in Mead House (where we both lived that freshman year), I also posted a note in the spirit of Schopenhauer, my favorite philosopher of the time: "The world is your will and idea."

I joined the college English Honors program that year after my composition teacher explained to me in the Blue Room (the coffee shop on the campus at Faunce House) that I could skip the second part of the composition course if I were willing to sign up for the English Honors program instead. I had not given much thought to what I might major in, but the program sounded reasonable to me; participating in small literature discussions around a table rather than listening to monologues in a large lecture hall had some appeal, I assumed. I did confess, though, that I would never become a literature professor. Yes, I was a mature and responsible young man in those days, no doubt. Or perhaps an idiot. I am eighty years old now, though, and am beginning to think that Socrates had it right: The beginning of wisdom comes when you realize you know nothing.

I suppose our poetry pamphlet *Echo Aonides* was actually what convinced me that I was on the right path in those days. It was well received by a few budding literary critics at the time. I grew a beard, let my hair grow long and wild, joined the literary rebels.

I don't want to talk about memory as nostalgia in these exchanges, but rather the way the past flows into the present—somewhat like Chagall's painting called *Time Is a River Without Banks*. It is in this sense that I enter (or help to rejuvenate) our friendship from those early days. I believe we can do that through language—open possibilities for what some might call the future. For me, though, this attempt at dialogue is not so much an attempt to create some linear sense of direction (past / present / future), but to add something to what has always been there. To try, in other words, to articulate what has always been "in-between" us. Or, to put it another way, to attempt to express something that is in "the gap," between what we know and what we cannot know, perhaps between the secular and the divine.

Yes, what we take to be apparently random events might very well be part of the destiny unique to our one and only precious life. If we had not renewed our friendship, we would not be engaged in this project, writing emails [henceforth called "letters"] to each other, focused on what appears to be  matters of shared interest and concern. Is this dialogue we are about to have an accident, or is it part of our destiny? That is  a question. I can only add to it, but certainly not answer it.

Random events?—Or facets of our destiny?

Language and imagination lead us on our way. If this conversation is an event of friendship then, it is perhaps, also, for us, an event of destiny. I could call it an act of remembrance that sets us in forward motion, or an addition to what has always been there but rarely turned to.

So, allow me now a few additional  questions in response to your letter. What about language itself? What do we really know

9

about it? To me, it is baffling, a challenge, often mysterious, poly-semous ("many-meaning," more so than even James Joyce could have realized). Literary language, in particular, seems always to say more than it knows. It is rewarding, but it has its complica-tions—and its dangers. To me, language keeps us alive, but it's al-ways risky business.

And what about the limits of language—language at the edge? But at the edge of what?

Does language connect to the sacred, or is it always entangled with devilish conceit and cunning?

In 1949, Adorno claimed it would be barbaric to write poetry after the Holocaust. But he later changed his mind, suggesting that language, even if corrupt, was still our best hope against the si-lence of the Horror. The unimaginable had been proven imagina-ble and made visible, and this Horror seemed beyond anything we had called "our humanity." If a poet dared to write about it, it could be voiced only as a howl of infinite suffering that too often intensified the pain. We could no longer create joy and beauty and remain honest to such a vision of the world. Instead, we had dis-ruption and horror to contend with, nihilism, disenchantment, and inevitable disappearance rather than hope. Reality, it seemed, had outstripped the literary imagination?

One hundred and fifty years before the Holocaust, the English Romantic poets celebrated rebellion and the joyous promise of the creative power of language and literature.

William Blake insisted that poets could create through the im-agination "visionary forms dramatic," perhaps the "apocalyptic humanism" you make reference to. For Blake, the flow of imagi-nation was a way of moving from fear to hope to illumination in contrast to suffering, affliction, and disappearance.

William Wordsworth, in a different mode, felt that through poetry we could experience "intimations of immortality," "the living life within"—at least momentarily. He called these mo-ments "spots of time," sources of exquisite joy available to anyone open to them.

Percy Bysshe Shelley, too, thought the poetry of the imagina-tion could bring us close to "the deep truth" of the universe, a deep truth which was by necessity imageless (according to Shelley), but not beyond human experience.

So we have many different ways of thinking about what might be called the relation between language and literature and the edge of human consciousness. But then I ask, What and where is this "edge"? Surely it is connected to the silence you refer to.

Silence for Wordsworth, as an example, is obviously not the silence of the Horror that Adorno or Steiner are thinking about. I consider it as some kind of "absence," one that language can only hint at. It is a "nothingness," but far from an emptiness. For Wordsworth and many other poets in the 19th century, it is "something else," something that could be considered sacred and cannot be fully named. At times, it might be "the living life within," the invisible flow of Nature itself, or the Perfect Form of the Neo-Platonists. It suggests all sorts of possibilities. And I like to believe in those possibilities, that "something else."

Silence can be "something else," both sacred and impossible to fully name

When reading Wordsworth—a poet who reminds the critic Lionel Trilling of a rabbi of sorts—I often think that those Wordsworthian moments recall the Hebrew notion of a transcendent God who cannot be named, the Unnamed Name. Is this precisely what Wordsworth intended? In a sense, that doesn't matter. I consider my reaction a kind of translation, not a misreading, over-reading, or over-thinking, but part of the dialogue necessary for reading serious literature. In fact, I think of all such reading as a complex kind of dialogue between writer and reader, an ongoing process of interaction and translation between two friends deepening their quest for human understanding.

Literature (and more generally, language) remains our best hope for humanity, but, even before the Holocaust, it is not surprising to see poets like Friederich Hölderlin giving up writing for silence; Arthur Rimbaud, giving up writing for direct action; Franz Kafka insisting that all his stories be destroyed; Gerard Manley Hopkins wondering whether writing poems was a sin, and so on. Had they given up on the creative power of literary language? Or simply acknowledged its limits?

Some of the reviews of my book *The Risk of Reading* suggested that only a handful of readers still believe that literature could help make us human. Perhaps these reviewers thought I should have been born in 1800. Yes, I still hold onto the old belief that literature can make a difference, that literature can hint at the possibility of the impossible, that nothingness is not empty but murmurs with sparks of life if we listen closely and respond accordingly. But even members of my old English department have their doubts.

There was a time when God or Nature inspired poets, serving as the foundation for poetry. Today silence (or the void) seems at the center. As Yeats said, "Things fall apart; the centre cannot hold / Mere anarchy is loosed upon the world." For many, the sacred has disappeared. Yet we still have questions fueling desire, and we have dialogue to keep those questions alive. And, yes, we also have the coldness of death, the corpse itself, to contend with. Eros vs. thanatos—to pretend to simplify the matter. Or is it the Voice vs. Silence? I agree with you, David: Silence has extraordinary power.

When the
sacred
disappears,
does silence—
or the void—
take its place?

"We will not go gently into that dark night." As you say, when you begin a poem, you do not break the silence, but you rebel against it. Like reading, writing is risky business. It is perhaps somewhat like the journey of Orpheus to the underworld, a visitation that could cost you your life—or create a song.

David, how close do you dare to get? Silence can destroy human life. As you rightly observe, silence often demands obedience and has overwhelming power. Ask Aaron's sons struck down in the inner sanctuary of the Jewish temple for getting too close to God. Ask the prisoner rotting away in solitary confinement until the stone walls of his cell completely close in on him. Yet as a serious poet you remain courageous and desirous, as well as vulnerable. And of course the quiet pleasure of sitting alone at a friend's pool surrounded by voiceless and stone-like cement has its own dangers.

But I imagine you are writing (and I am reading). Imagining this helps keep me alive. I look to your poem, whose beginning immediately evokes particular interest for me: Music sets all in motion. I am mindful of the "unheard melodies" in John Keats's "Ode on a Grecian Urn," the unfolding of time in a different key, music from another place—like the song of a nightingale, perhaps, a remembrance in the present moment of what was, a vision of what could be. I don't hear that song very often these days, but, yes, through the opening of your poem, that first line, it already breathes with anticipation. It moves against the monstrous demands of a fearsome silence. "And so I return to music . . . "

And then I sense a calling for a pause at the end of this opening line, a hesitation of the breath that allows silence for a moment to embody itself in the language, to yield some of its nihilistic power to the articulation of the sound of the song itself. For me, this pause at the end of the poem's opening line vibrates, transforms into further courage for you the poet, and me the reader, turning the power of silence into the rhythm of living experience, the breath of ongoing temporal movement. As you suggest in the poem, you (the poet) can now spot the blue ripples rejoicing in the liquid flow of life as they kiss that hard concrete walkway. And then you can continue on, incomplete and mortal, as you must be, walking upright, with the language of the world surrounding you, helping you to envision a new creation, coming and going, despite the silence. Those blue ripples remain within the reader's heart as well—a kiss that at least for a time allows something more than hard concrete to block the flow and movement of life itself.

Like mortal life, your poem, still just beginning, can go off in many directions, and I want to join your rebellion. But I don't anticipate the poem will ever be fully complete, fully closed off—no, it will not end as a photographic picture, without movement, permanently framed and nailed on my wall. Instead, it will do what literature does best, inspire by raising questions, allow me as a reader to continue on my quest, refresh me with its blue ripples of possibilities experienced through the language. It is a call inviting response.

Literature can give us an ongoing choice, a kind of freedom that offers hope. But it does not provide answers. As Milan Kundera says about the novel (and we could say the same about poetry): "A novel does not assert anything. A novel searches and poses questions." By contrast, he adds, "the totalitarian world is a world of answers rather than questions." So, perhaps at the edge of literature, the engaged reader discovers a moment of freedom and responsibility—a kiss sending us on another quest. It reminds us of both our coming and our going. It is a surprise.

What literature does best: it asks questions and inspires us to continue our quest

And suddenly there is another surprise for me, your reader. I uncovered something about our undergraduate poetry pamphlet that I had never realized before. Would it have ever happened without this exchange of letters between friends? When Edwin Honig, the resident poet at Brown when we were undergraduates there, wrote the introduction to our poetry pamphlet, he claimed (with much generosity), "Waxler's work is full of prophetic, Blakean muscle . . . his ballads . . . move in the dark . . . enjoying their superrealistic firelights, clanging with 'streetcar fantasies of playful truth.'"

It was only today that I realized that that bit of linguistic rambling, circulating around in my unconscious all these years, was probably the silent spark that led me to my love for William Blake! Was that silence, embedded in Honig's language all these years, slowly manifesting itself through decades of my life?

As a graduate student, I wrote my dissertation on Blake under the mentorship of David Erdman (a leading Blake scholar at the time), and I later gave my oldest son Jonathan the middle name Blake, believing in the power of Jonathan's imagination. I doubt Honig realized the role his words played in my life. Yet I believe now that Honig's words made a profound difference for me. Perhaps that is the way language works? It always knows more than it says.

So, I now return to your discussion of Blake's "Tyger."

As I write now, I realize that I have entered into a dialogue and a type of translation not only with your poem but with your letter as a whole. Another uplifting surprise. Your comments on Blake's "Tyger" (and its link to "the apocalyptic moment") silently resonate with your poem: yes, I begin to think about the moment of creation and/or destruction; if not revelation, at least something to be questioned about hope and fear, life and death.

**How much risk do we dare to take?**

Your comments about Blake's "Tyger" raise an important question: How close (proximity) or how far away (distance) do we want to be in relation to the tiger? How much risk do we want to take—as mortal human beings, as readers, as poets, as speakers of language? I sense that this particular tiger, with its yellow and black stripes, radiant and open to us, is filled with light and exudes sublime beauty, a Blakean illumination. He is not in a cage, not behind bars. But how close do we dare to get? How close should we get? Surely distance and perspective are required. Is this sublime radiance a protection against death or is it a profound danger that haunts us from some unknown place? Will it lead us to freedom or to disappearance? In its own way, your poem seems to start asking similar questions.

And there is, as well, the revolutionary tiger for Blake, as there is your rebellion against the silence at the beginning of your poem.

To George III, the king of England at the time, the tiger is understandably frightening (the king might lose his head!). But to revolutionaries like Blake, the tiger is filled with hope and vision. So what position do we take? Those are questions not only for the reader but also for the speaker (the writer), the poet himself. In one sense, the reader becomes the writer, who dares to risk the possible revelation, the singularity of the moment when creation and destruction are uncovered as such, as if the power and beauty of the tiger could bring us to the edge of the world and transform it. I note though that Blake keeps the questions wide open in this poem, indicating that this "song of experience" (as Blake called it) is not the end, but part of an ongoing journey. Are we, readers and speakers, first and foremost questioners on a quest, called to the belief in the poetic imagination and its infinite possibilities?

> Did he smile his work to see?
> Did he who made the Lamb make thee?
>
> . . .
>
> What immortal hand or eye
> Dare frame thy fearful symmetry?

These lines from Blake bring me back again to your poem. What are some of the questions embedded there? How will they unfold?

> And so I return to music by the pool
> and watch the water's blue ripples
> kiss and kiss again the pool's concrete walkway.
>
> The sun passes overhead, eyes the pool,
> extends down transparent fingers to touch
> the ripples as if he owns them
> at least to nightfall

Thanks to you, David, my imagination (your reader) continues the desire to quest on.

Nightfall sends the sun away! Okay. But isn't the sun, even at night, always there? So does nightfall really send it away, or does our mortality limit our perceptions, make us blind to possibilities beyond our sense of limitations? Your sun seems to me, right now anyway, to have a lot in common with the tiger! How close do we want to get to that sun anyway? Does it offer a solar kiss (for those splendid blue ripples) or is it engaged in a dangerous act of potential violence? Is this illumination or violence? Does the way the sun eyes the pool suggest a desiring predator or a compassionate friend? "A solar embrace or an act of ownership?" And what about nightfall? Is the silence and darkness of the coming night something to be feared or embraced? Is it friend or foe? For the moment, I leave the questions as they are. Some things to wonder about.

As for the issues of poetry versus prose, speaking versus writing, again you offer in your discussion a number of thoughtful insights. I think your suggestion that our dialogue be considered "written poetry" is applicable to your side of the dialogue, although I am not sure I qualify in that category. But I like the idea. Of course, there's nothing like face-to-face conversation, especially with some good wine, but I agree that written poetry is a strong substitute. And how could I not agree with you when you say that the real culprits when it comes to silence and the Holocaust are those, like the Nazi criminals, who remained silent until the bitter end?

I am also reminded that polysemous language (especially literature, whether poetry or prose) indicates (to me at least) that we are always with another, that we are, in other words, never alone. There is a doubleness in literature, a telling as a retelling, an experience of the present on the one side and a reflection on the past which points to possibility in the future on the other side. We are always talking to another, whether that other is just ourself, some imagined reader, or an actual listener. In this context, too, as you have suggested, the use of language is, at times, an act of rebellion against the power of silence. But what is the silence here in your poem—is it the sun as a desiring predator? Or is it the dark night that might protect us from blindness and disappearance? Perhaps it is the concrete walkway itself: It has no voice, only a fixed and silent gaze, a cement slab of death. Surely it's not that compassionate sun which warmed the blue ripples of water before it was sent packing at nightfall—or is it?

Bob

# 4. Friendship Keeps Us Alive

Bob,

Before moving to your comments on language, and their inevitable path to literature, I want to speak to the third element in our subtitle: friendship. Being devotees of the Word, I'm tempted to come up with a working definition and run it by you for, what else?—discussion. But that feels bloodless. No, it's all the elusive, undefinable treats of our friendship that I want to acknowledge here. Who wrote, "There is nothing lost that cannot be found, if sought"? For me, losing our undergraduate friendship, and reviving an adult version now, informs our letters start to finish. Thank you for being my friend.

To language: Your musings are spot-on for me. Most intriguing: "Language seems to know more than it says." As you say, it is literary language you refer to here. May I expand our rumination to spoken as well as literary language? How do they differ?

In antiquity, I wonder if they did differ. In Homer's time, epics were spoken (or sung), and made their way to print after the fact. Some think Homer may have dictated them to a scribe. Was it at that juncture that written language indeed became literary? Previous to it, did singers construct their performances on the spot, spontaneously, or did they write texts and then commit them to memory? If the former (as with, say, modern improvisational theatre troupes), was it true spoken language, and therefore free of the strictures and weight of literary ambitions and texts?

Does this help us to throw into relief the condition of language itself, to plumb the idea that *language knows more than it says*?

Coming forward to our time, the age of the unconscious, this seems a truism. If I stand on a street corner and shout, "Down with the government," surely these words know more than they say because the subtext, housing why, for me, the government must fall, is withheld, and raises the question, Do I really know why I say this? Have I analyzed the government and seen that it's so inept that it must fall, or am I simply acting out resentment of authority figures, going back to my father?

To turn your phrase on its head (or its side), what if language says more than it knows? This may be the more intriguing question, indicating a common dilemma. Given that nearly everyone, in every culture, speaks at a very young age—indeed, at an age when reason is absent—can't we say that the language spoken then "says more than it knows"? If a child of, say, three, says "Down with the government," she surely knows little or nothing about what she says. She must, we think, be parroting what's she heard, and can't be held responsible.

Reverting to your thoughts on the English Romantics and their "celebrated rebellion and the joyous promise of the creative power of language and literature," I'm struck that in our letters now, that joyous promise is very much what you and I are about. What we have, of course, that the Romantics did not, is the overlay of modernism: all that's happened since their era—widespread public education, the rise of democracies, the power of science and technologies, the traumas of the Holocaust and other atrocities—and the effects of all these on language. If Adorno is right, that it is barbaric to write poetry after the Holocaust (or, he might have added, after Hiroshima), then what of all the poetry and literature that has been written since?

And what of us? Are we barbaric to spend our lives as we have, looking for the good and the beautiful in language and literature, and celebrating it when we find it? My answer, self-serving and irrational, is No.

I throw in with Shelley and his faith that poetry and imagination can bring us "the deep truth" of the universe, though I'd alter it (in a way that would probably make Shelley aghast) to say that the deep truth language can lead us to is that of ourselves. This is Jungian for sure, positing that to know the self is to know the universe.

And Waxlerian, in its faith that literature remains our best hope for humanity. Again, to alter things a bit (and hope this does not leave *you* aghast) I might eschew the superlative and say that literature remains a viable hope for humanity. It's the furthest I can go. Whether you agree with my stance or not, I am in full harmony with you on how imagination and writing helps keep us alive.

And, as are you, I'm fully with Kundera that literature's business (and I'd add, its glory) is to ask questions, while the totalitarian world is full of answers.

I quite love your thoughts on my poem, and particularly the line that nightfall "sends [the sun] packing." And I love the fact that your thinking takes the form of questions—more, that you show full faith in the proposition that questions, not answers, are true pathways to . . . what? Why, to what our exchanges yearn for: truth, enlightenment, friendship.

But I must halt for now, as I see I have just erred by positing answers.

David

# 5. Forging Ahead

## David,

I took a third Covid shot the other day, and that knocked me back to bed for a while. Am recovered and confident to forge ahead now.

I had not given much thought recently to George Steiner until you mentioned him, but certainly the Holocaust and its aftermath are crucial to our thinking about the relation of language and literature to the ineffable. Steiner helps with this. What are the limits of language in its pursuit of "something more"? What is the relationship between the secular word and silence? Between the secular word and the divine word? Is there a gap between the secular word and the divine word—one that the poet works to fill?

Can the Bible give us insight into the post-modern version of such questions? Or are all such questions today irrelevant?

I have been looking at the creation scenes in Genesis, for example, in terms of the language of creation ("Let there be light"), in terms of the breath of inspiration bringing life to the red clay, in terms of the gift of language given to Adam in naming the animals, and so on. In this context, I have also read some of the commentary from the Talmud and Kabbalah. Was there a "perfect language" lost through the so-called Fall of Adam and Eve? Or even before the Tower of Babel? Can poets and writers recover that language, renew it now, or is it much too late? Is it at best, a mythic dream? Did the Holocaust close out all such possibilities?

In the midst of my reading, I have also discovered a number of modern thinkers (Thorlief Boman, Susan Handelman, Marléna Zarader, Lev Shestov, Edmond Jabès, Yoram Hazony) who discuss the often-overlooked difference between the Hebrew word *davar* and the Greek word *logos*. I see this sense of difference as an opening to possibilities. I take my lead on much of this from Boman, although his work is admittedly controversial, but, in my view, not disproven. The same could be said about Handelman, Zarader, Shestov, Hazony, and Jabès. I want to use these words (*davar* and *logos*) as what I think of as a kind of probe into issues of particular concern to me (and others, I hope), issues that call for dialogue. I admit that at times I will find it necessary to generalize (perhaps over-generalize), but I want to make it clear here that what I say is mainly a suggestion, a way of moving forward, all done in the spirit of dialogue. I dream next to the words I write. And I acknowledge anything said could have been different.

For example, the Hebrew word *davar* ( first appearing in Genesis 11) means "word" but also "act" and "thing." It has a polysemous quality to it. To me, it suggests promise rather than something already visible, movement rather than contemplation, a connectivity or relationship ( a cleavage rather than an essence). In terms of history, I would suggest *davar* is related to the present as possibility and responsibility for work not yet complete but ongoing. By contrast, the Greek word *logos* is closely associated with reason and logic and the story of Jesus as Christ, a universal perfection in its totality and completion. I want to explore this difference as we broaden our discussion.

In this context, when John begins his Gospel, "The Word was God, and the Word was with God" (often referred to as the "Hymn to Logos"), he might very well be thinking about both *davar* and *logos*. But, in either case, John hints at a duality, an oscillation of the Word: God as the Word, God and the Word. John sets in motion an oscillation that cannot easily be stopped. Reading the "Hymn to Logos," it is as if the reader can see (perhaps for the first time) the oscillation between the flesh and the spirit. The flesh, we might say, is potentially separate from the spirit. It is as if the power of the eye is evoked, the visual comes into view. Such language begins over a long period of historical time in the

West to separate and complicate the relationship between the literal and the spiritual, the body and the soul, faith and reason, word and object—a duality that the Hebrews did not seem to experience as such, but a duality that has monumental significance as it develops what we usually call Western civilization.

Perhaps the church fathers see this even more clearly. Even the charitable Augustine seems, at times, to be saying that the literal word is dead (the "Old Testament") and the spiritual word alone is now alive (the "New Testament"). In this regard, we seem to be moving from a world of Law and the Book to a world of grace and the flesh. (Good news for some, but not so much for the Jews.)

For background, let me note the strong emphasis among the Jews in terms of language and the Book ("the People of the Book"), a belief in the ongoing study of the Book not only as the Law but also as the enactment of the deeds (*mitzvah*) and stories inscribed with the Law onto their hearts (where, for them, knowledge resides). Modern scholars like Abraham Heschel will even say that the stories in the Hebrew Bible are more important than the Law itself. The word and the act are joined together. I contrast this with a growing appreciation for the visible (statues, monuments, buildings in Greece and Rome and in the churches as they develop after Jesus). Does this mark a difference in consciousness as well? Seeing privileged over listening, for example? The eye rather than the ear? Perhaps even an emphasis on the foreground rather than the invisible background in stories, stories that affect the way we think about reality. As Auerbach brilliantly discusses it in his monumental essay called "Odysseus' Scar."

Following Auerbach, Geoffrey Hartman in *The Third Pillar* makes a similar point about the differences between Hebraic stories and Hellenic stories. Preserving certain cultural similarities, he nevertheless emphasizes the differences. As he puts it in his opening chapter, "Struggle for the Text":

> By comparing two passages, the Akedah from the Bible and a recognition scene from the nineteenth book of the Odyssey—passages that do not have the slightest thematic relation—and by refusing to disqualify one to the light of the

*Stories and the Law, the word and the act: all inextricably intertwined*

23

other, or to find the same basic structure in them, Auerbach maintains a gap between Scripture and fiction, if only in the form of Hebraic versus Hellenic.

I am looking for differences, as I have said, rather than similarities, although, like Hartman, I want to underline my commitment to the importance of similarities as well. Yet I need to ask: Do these differences also suggest a new and ongoing need for translation as well? I think we can agree that the Hebrew Bible is read in a very different way once it is changed to the so-called Old Testament and once it is translated into Greek and Latin, for example. This is why even Augustine in his discussion about how to read suggests at one point that Cain be read as the Jew, Abel as the precursor for Jesus. No doubt this is support for allegorical readings, but it is also a reminder of the polysemous quality of the Hebrew Bible. How do we read? What is the nature of language itself? We might ask.

The early discussions about words, language, and literature in Greek philosophy are also relevant here. The most famous example is probably Plato in *The Republic* when he wants to kick out all the poets, those copiers of copies, craftsman too distant from the Perfect Forms. The whole notion of how words "represent" things seems to be raised by Plato here and carried through Western Civilization. As Plato puts it, "And the tragic poet is an imitator, and therefore, like all other imitators, he is twice removed from the king and from the truth."

Plato's *Cratylus* is another significant discussion about language. It raises the important question whether words are based on convention—in other words, arbitrary—or whether they are natural, somehow connected with what they supposedly represent.

By contrast with Plato, Aristotle defends the poets as artists and claims that poetry combines the particular with the universal, thus making "a concrete universal" (as some critics call it). As a reader, I generally find myself more in sympathy with Aristotle on such matters, although Aristotle is often a little too mathematical, too systematic for me. His defense of Greek tragedy cannot be outdone, although even there I would suggest that his chosen example (*Oedipus Rex*) is not necessarily the most typical example of Greek tragedy but the best for Aristotle's own definitions.

So, we have Hebrew versus Greek, *davar* versus *logos* as matters to explore more fully in our ongoing dialogue.

In thinking about the limits of language, the path from Longinus to Edmund Burke also deserves a quick mention, and then especially the two generations of the English Romantics. But here, too, a fundamental question remains unresolved for me. Can language and literature express (or discover) something unthinkable, something ineffable? Something beyond the threshold, beyond its own subjective making? Does the knowledge offered by language reduce its power or enhance it? (Perhaps this is part of the question that Yeats raises in "Leda and the Swan": "Did she put on his knowledge with his power/Before the indifferent beak could let her drop?") Or, to put it another way, does language say more than it knows?

Language, literature, and the ineffable

Many modern writers and poets work with these issues: Charles Baudelaire and his spleen, Rimbaud and his attempts at the derangement of the senses, Stéphane Mallarmé and his creation of "pure music," Samuel Beckett in his last book *The Unnameable*. Modern Jewish writers are also interested in the relationship between language and nothingness or silence.

In our old college days, I didn't realize that this nothingness is part of a tradition going back to the Hebrew Bible and the Kabbalah, in which God withdraws from the world but leaves fragments and sparks of possibility for humans to work with in order to repair the broken world—*tikkun olam*. But today I often think about those divine sparks and fragments of possibility. Maybe too many people think about silence and nothingness as the kind of empty silence created by fascism and Nazism, the kind of silence and nihilism formed out of hatred and fascination, usually driven by fear and the longing for brute power. I think antisemitism is a perfect example of such wrong-headed thinking, whether it be fascism, Nazism, or conspiracy theories in general.

If I am right in my belief that language and literature can make a difference, surely they must play a role in helping us to rebel against this form of silencing. But I must ask: Is it possible to hear the whisper of a silence that surpasses human

25

understanding but yet touches the heart and inspires a kiss? I think it is possible.

Bob

# 6. Whom We Write For

Bob,

Thanks for your last; I feel you fully engaged and energized. Ah, the doubleness of literature. It conjures the Yeatsian dialogue of self and soul, Wordsworth's conversation with himself in his long poems. And Eliot's

> . . . these things that with myself I too much
> discuss, too much explain.

And as you say, "we are, in the act of writing, always with another . . . never alone." What comfort in this. And further: "whether that other is just ourself, some imagined reader, or an actual listener."

Three possibilities: writing just for oneself, for an imagined reader, or for an actual one. I wonder, in regard to more solitary writers (Thoreau, Dickinson, Rilke), which of the three they posited, consciously or otherwise. As to myself, commercial work was always for an actual reader (usually, my boss!). But poetry—I confess, I don't really know.

Playwrights can have a leg up in this in that plays are communal and community activities (though many a playwright works alone, with only her characters for company).

To pursue the thought of who we write for, Bob, we are lucky that we are friends. A literary friendship is something to be valued, and since we've reconnected, I revel in ours. It means that we each provide the other with a ready ear and mind, not to judge the other's thoughts and words, but to receive and honor them. Isn't this a unique kind of freedom?

Sure, we are, as humans, judging animals, yet that's far from all we are. As friends I think we have *chosen* to support and appreciate what the other has to say. Both of us benefit. Yes, we were schooled as writers to fully expect critiques, and as readers to give them, but here, I hope, we attain a higher level of discourse—one more akin to offering and hearing new music.

But to revert to Adorno, I went back to his assertion that it would be barbaric to write poetry after the Holocaust, and I think it resonates in this context. Yet his stance, that we should forego writing, would disrupt the relationship of self to self or self to another, and so further the human drive toward separateness, even silence. Is this why Adorno changed his mind later?

Writing as an essential act of connection

I want to take up another early thought of yours: the relation of language to the ineffable. You ask: "Was there a 'perfect language' lost through the so-called Fall of Adam and Eve?—Or even before the Tower of Babel? Can poets and writers recover that language, renew it now, or is it much too late?"

Surely this question comes from a deep and urgent place. For if, as claimed in Genesis, at one time all people spoke one language, and all understood one another, then they were indeed in a paradise, not just of language but of spirit. Given that, how can we not look back and yearn for such a condition? I do want to dwell on that. Being in a posture of looking back at any perceived golden age makes certain demands on the psyche, one being that we by definition come after, and are "fallen." Then, of course, we can argue that we are in need of salvation or at the least enlightenment, perhaps desperately so. Is this a subtext we moderns must live with?

I'm thinking particularly of the subjectivity, absurdity, futility, and anarchy that early modernist writers felt compelled to employ or come to grips with, that we inherited and must adhere to, or ignore at our peril.

Now, alienation due to industrialization, not to mention World War I, were huge factors for our grandfathers and their Lost Generation. But what of us? Can we look back at them as being in the golden Age (feels like a major misnomer) of alienation, whereas we are stuck with second-hand angst?

Back to the ineffable. Do we apply the term to what can't be spoken of morally or spiritually (implying prohibition, not necessarily inability), or that for which we have simply no vocabulary and so can't speak of even if we wish? If the latter, we have to come to grips with ever-evolving insight.

Before Chaucer, was there the capacity to put language to a rich narrative of pilgrimage blending humor, desire, and quirky characters?

Before Shakespeare, was there any capacity to ruminate, in such layered fashion, on suicide, as Hamlet does?

Before Hemingway, did anyone think, much less express, how "pretty" it would be for a wounded warrior to think of a future with an unobtainable lover?

And before Freud, who could even think about the power of the unconscious, much less locate it in his living, breathing contemporaries, and write deeply of its implications?

So, is the ineffable a temporary blockage continually being pushed forward, as past 10-yard stakes along a football field?

Your analysis of the pool poem is sharp and insightful, and it sets me thinking. I sense that my poem comes from a primitive place where the sun is understood to ride across the sky and disappear until dawn. Why is this? Perhaps because we've posited silence as a malevolent force, a view in itself premodern, even atavistic. (This rather than silence as a beneficial balm or respite from noise, or, as the Quakers have it, a holy thing, a condition for the inward embrace of the Divine.) Given this, I'm intrigued that the poem's cosmology harkens back to a pre-Copernican, even pre-Aristotelian place. That I say this in full knowledge that the poem is mine feels both awkward and, well, spacey.

To keep it going:

> The sun, before fleeing, paints the ripples'
> peaks with blue and orange light, while
> drawing from them a like response,
> inner-lit and inner-derived, and born of some
> barely tamed spirit in love only with giving
> briefest life to rhythmic wet.

The great writers, continually pushing back the boundaries of the ineffable

Incidentally, you must have noticed, as I have, that the "music" of the poem's first line—that "to which I return"—has not been dealt with or paid out. A flaw? I can hear someone asking just that in a poetry workshop. What to do?

David

# 7. A Walk, Not a Sprint

David,

L ooks like a walk rather than sprint or jog, as you like to say. But Thoreau, for one, knew how important walking is. Once the legs get going, the whole body flows, from head to toe. The heart pumps, and the brain lights up. Or is it the mind working at full capacity? Well, in Thoreau's case anyway.

I am struck by your discussion of how language evolves as we experience it through literature; and as language evolves, we move closer and closer to the goal line of knowledge and under-standing. I used to embrace that notion wholeheartedly, along with the progressive liberal belief in the political context—but now I am not so sure. In my mind, literature can create new hori-zons for the reader, so we can see what we had not seen previously, and we can compare/contrast that new horizon with the old hori-zon. But whether there is evolution here (or movement toward the goal line) remains a question for me now. It is perhaps a little like asking why Moses could not enter the Promised Land. As Kafka put it, it was not because his life was too short, or because he was being punished for breaking the tablets, but because he was a human being. As Kafka, borrowing from the rabbis, no doubt knew, you are not required to complete the work, but neither are you free to desist from it.

For me, this is a responsibility given in different ways to all of us, a gift to remind us of the one unique precious life granted to us. And I find within that responsibility a question that always moves me. The poet Mary Oliver put it this way:

Doesn't everything die at last and too soon?
Tell me, what is it that you plan to do
With your one wild and precious life?

Incomplete
and anxious—
the human
condition

Perhaps Freud was right when he suggested that ambivalence was at the root of human life. In this sense, we are incomplete and anxious: filled with trauma from the beginning, struggling between eros and thanatos, often discontented with civilization and its supposed necessity. This is a continuing narrative, succession as displacement, but it is not just the son attempting to displace the father (as Freud seems to have argued), but also the combat of brothers (or sisters) as sibling rivalry (as Freud also suggested). Literature and language, a kind of talking cure, can make a difference. But the cure is always the poison, too. This is probably what Plato, ambivalent about poets and poetry, had in mind. And doesn't it seem more reasonable to think that anxiety (which Adam seems to have had long before Eve appeared) causes repression, rather than repression causing anxiety? Did God realize that Adam could not be alone?

I'd say that what we conventionally call *evolution* is not so much related to progress but to what we turn towards and what we turn away from—at least when I focus on difference (rather than on the universal sense of the same). I see evolution as a matter of subtraction and addition rather than progress, I suppose. Surely we are creatures, just as animals are, but it is language, with all its complexity and tensions, that makes us what we are. Language separates us from the other creatures of the world as we spin the words we live in to explore possibilities, attempting not simply to create joy and communication, but communion with the world; yet also protecting ourselves from our own death, the death that cannot be voiced.

To me, that spinning of words does not indicate a dull round, an endless circle heading to the same place it started from, but a kind of digging (to change the metaphor), a tuning and turning again, a turning up of new ground, Call it evolution if you like, but I think it is a matter of turning towards a gift to help us move onwards in our one precious life—or perhaps a way of taking responsibility to discover our individual story before its ending discovers

32

us. Driven by inquisitiveness, we turn toward the other, not so much for an answer, but as a way to continue the quest and the question—that is, to glimpse for a moment our place within the creative act of communion.

As a Jewish joke goes: "Why, my friend, do you spend so much time asking questions?"

"Why not?

At times, such turning might begin with a simple touch—the touch of books on a library shelf, for example. More than seventy years have gone by, but it might just as well be today. As we often did, my mother and I are walking from our home through the newly cut green grass at Buttonwood Park in New Bedford. There is a branch library there, small tables with chairs for reading, all sizes of books sorted by categories on the shelves of the four walls. Turning towards those shelves, I touch a book from the section marked *fiction*, look at the colors on the cover as I brush it gently with my right hand, slowly open the pages, and glance at the printed words. "I'd like to take this book home," I tell my mother. "I'd like to read it." And I did. All before we gathered for supper that night.

Remembering the physical touch of a book

An unexplained touch deeply embedded in a cell in my body over seventy years ago opens now not as a distant past memory, but as a call today, perhaps another moment of destiny sending me along the way. I dare say it seems close to what some might call the immemorial past, perhaps a silent fragment of unknown time turning through my mother into my body at the moment of conception.

So, in terms of your poem as it develops: I'd say it spins (and turns), just as you might say it evolves. It is both, I suppose. And that is part of the wonder of dialogue and friendship.

I see now that the sun takes on further and deeper light. It too has its destiny and its ambivalence. It seemed ominous earlier, in some ways predatory, but now, it seems to move from its previous visual gaze to a heightened sense of inspired giving and sensuous rhythm—and I feel that kiss running through the whole poem now.

But then, near the end of your last letter, you comment, "Incidentally, you must have noticed, as I have, that the music of the poem's first line, that 'to which I return,' has not been dealt with or paid out. A flaw? I can hear someone asking just that in a poetry workshop. What to do?"

Yes, I did wonder about that music when I first read your poem. But now the music in the poem itself seems in part to solve the issue—as if the music heard from somewhere else is internalized in the poem as it unfolds. It is sound that gives the poem its magic (or let's say its literary merit). Perhaps this is true of all literature, but certainly of poetry. So the voice (and the ear) become crucial in this regard. A kind of tension between the solar orb and the spirit in love? But perhaps the music you heard sitting at the pool was the same song that Ruth heard—that is, the song of the nightingale (as Keats would have it), or the music without notes from the "Ode on a Grecian Urn"—the rhythm of the imagination itself.

But why at a friend's pool, surrounded by cement? Could the music be from a radio nearby? Are we in the modern world here, maybe even the suburbs? Or is the reader dreaming next to the poem as it unfolds?

Bob

# 8. Breaking Silence: Adam and God

Bob,

O ne of my favorite times is right now, reading, rereading, and digesting what you've written, absorbing your thought, your language, backed by Kafka, Freud, Keats et al.—their thought and language enriching ours.

We, poised on the poles of eros and thanatos, here on Hamlet's "bank and shoal of time."

On instinct, I just turned to the book of Genesis for a reread. Chapter one, verse five: "God called the light day, and the darkness, night." First reactions: Assuming that God spoke these words aloud, they are the first words to be given voice in the Bible. God has broken silence!

Then Adam follows suit, at 2:20, naming everything—fowls and beasts. Words spoken, where before there were none?

Continuing, at 3:9, God asks Adam, "Where art thou?" Immediately, 3:10, Adam answers, "I heard thy voice in the garden."

How did Adam recognize God's voice? Had he ever heard another voice? If so, whose? What was Adam's relationship with language? And what language? Clearly the same one God spoke. How did he learn it?

Soon, God and Adam get downright loquacious. It's an out-and-out talk-fest about Eve, good and evil, and so on.

But let's go back to God breaking silence. Of course, the first words in 1:1 are "In the beginning." But the beginning of what? Clearly there was an earlier beginning, as God already exists at this point. For how long had he been silent? Eons, an eternity? It begs the question, what is God's history pre-Adam and Eve? The immense silence God lived with then: how does this fit into our discussion? Was this silence a burden for him? And of course, who created God to begin with? Is he self-created? The mind backs away, doubts itself, then reasserts its right to know.

After Genesis, the Bible has much to do with silence, and most of it is positive. Psalm 62: "For God alone, O my soul, wait in silence, for my hope is from him." Ecclesiastes 3:7-8: "a time to tear and a time to sew; a time to be silent and a time to speak." Or Psalm 141:3: "O Lord, set a guard at my mouth. Keep watch over the door of my lips."

Here is a fervent prayer to stay silent.

I may be starting to see the limits of our proposition that silence is a tyrant. What to do? I'm stopped by your sharing of the rabbinic wisdom: "You are not required to complete the work, but neither are you free to desist from it." How about Ulysses and the sirens in Kafka's "The Silence of the Sirens"? In putting wax in his own ears (rather than those of his shipmates, as in Homer's version), Kafka's Ulysses seeks silence instead of keeping his ears open while lashing himself to the mast so he can hear the Siren's songs and survive.

Which would you choose? As for me, I'd want to hear those songs and survive, perhaps to tell to others their seductive qualities. But then I've always loved the notion of "coming back to tell you all," be it Coleridge's Ancient Mariner singling out the wedding guests to hear his cautionary tale, or Melville's Ishmael surviving the wreck of the *Pequod*, saying "I only am escaped alone to tell thee."

This breaking of silence is of another order, words spoken to affirm life. Does this bring us back to our thesis: that breaking silence is a way of rebelling, defying the tyrant in order to give life?

Per your question about the "music by the pool" in the poem: Its source is unspecified, but I think it is an internal music, one that the speaker has unknowingly brought with him, and which gets activated here, by this pool, very much because the surrounding cement is so hard, unforgiving, non-acoustical, so that the music, the heretofore "unheard melodies," must break its silence or die.

David

# 9. Does Creation Emerge Out of Nothing?

David,

Wat is that sound of silence which you begin to trace in the Biblical text? Does creation emerge out of nothing (*ex nihilo*), or does it inform the chaos already at hand? Does God create as a poet might—through the word—or is He more like a potter, giving shape to the clay? Is it the mouth or the hand, the ear or the eye that we should privilege? Or are they both of equal merit?

I used to think that poetry was naming and had a normative function—that it was primarily an attempt to bring together, unify. It was also a way of shaping the clay to be seen. Now I think it is more to do with separation, difference, an attempt to distinguish one person / thing from another. Poetry is not about the perfect circle, or the peace and harmony of heaven, or the ideal Platonic form, nor should it be considered a monologue (which always threatens to inspire a demagogue). Instead, poetry begins with a poet leaning forward, straining to hear another voice before he begins, then straining to speak, to give voice to what some have called "the unvocalized voice," so that the listener might be willing to lean forward as well, to stretch to hear and try to understand. Not monologue but ongoing dialogue, a multitude of voices to be interpreted and responded to.

The poet does not write to fully convert the reader or the world. What he wants is to give voice to that which cannot be fully

Poetry as dialogue

communicated—call it silence?—the part of the world that has not been named or translated, the unwritten. It is in this sense that the poem at its best cannot be anything other than what it is, a singularity, an original, without end or absolute, definitive meaning.

I now have a clearer understanding of why Blake downplayed memory, insisting on creation and imagination. Memory is often incorrectly considered as a call for distance, an attempt to copy, a way of making the past into a commodity; even the Muses become echoes (*Echo Aonides?*). Instead of the immediacy of creation and the play of the freedom of imagination—the existential experience in movement and action—too often the use of memory is mere adaptation and copying, abstraction and formulas, all kinds of strategies to stop the flow of thinking and playful enchantment. For Blake, the world can be experienced in a grain of sand because the possibilities of enchantment and creation are always present and always endless, calling us to move ahead—to listen and to act. For Blake, then, memory is not mere recollection of picture images from a distant past—that is, a nostalgic retreat into an illusion, an abstraction that blocks the flow of breath, of human life. Rather, memory is remembrance as it pushes its way into the  present moving towards the future: *zakhor* (the Hebrew for "remembrance"), as the historian Yoself Yerushalmi explains it.

In his foreword to *Zakhor*, the groundbreaking book by the historian Yosef Hayim Yerushalmi, Harold Bloom makes the important point for us: There is a particular Hebrew psychology of memory, Bloom insists. *Zakhor*, as a word, has a much wider range than "recollection" in English. In Hebrew, remembrance is not to re-collect but to act, to do—parallel to the Hebrew *davar*, often translated as *logos* but meaning "act" and "thing" and "word." Its polysemous quality resonates as a verb (with a copula attached), a word that summons us to responsibility and communal action.

But I also wonder what is our uniqueness, each one of us. I remember idolizing Martin Luther King, Jr., at one time, and I said to my father, "I wish I could stir the crowds to help create equality and freedom like MLK does." In reply, my father said something like, "If God ever meets you at the pearly gates, He will not ask you why you were not more like MLK, but why you were not more like Bob Waxler."

I admire that. But what is that uniqueness? The who rather than the what? Perhaps, as the poets often say, it is our unique pain, pain that struggles for justice and beauty? But also the pain that occurs when we acknowledge the impossibility of describing the experience of our own unique death, the experience that cannot be communicated or even articulated. Is that the deep core of all our loneliness and loss? And is this why I prefer dialogue (rather than monologue), why we were given the gift of language in the first place? Each poem is an event, disrupting death, but then falling back into silence, yet singular in its sacrifice and mourning. A kind of generous lie, a fiction that is the only truth we, as humans, can know. Even if we seek the "what" of essence, we also strive for connection with the other, the one who is always waiting for us.

At the Passover seder, for example, Jews do not recollect their slavery in Egypt as if it were long ago and far distant from the promise of the present. Instead, they open themselves through word and ritual to the remembrance of suffering and freedom— the past flowing into the present and the future in every generation, letting each person regard him or herself in their eachness as though now emerging from Egypt. And so it is enacted each year at the Passover seder, with the language of the contemporary world giving it additional purpose and direction.

Viewed in this way, every poem is, in some sense, a success, but also a failure, never defeating death, but continuing to offer hope. This is probably what Beckett means when he says: "Fail, fail again, fail better." As the rabbis say, we are not required to finish the work, but we are obligated to continue it. The French Revolution, the Paris Commune, the Occupy movement were all failures in one sense. But tied into those very failures was hope, hope that continues on, not hope as a reaction to failure, but hope emerging with the movement of the failure itself. It is, to me, a little like Coleridge complaining that "Kubla Khan" is a failure, incomplete and hopeless, because a businessman from Porlock interrupted his dreaming by knocking on his door. Imagine how many have taken hope and enchantment from this supposed failure.

Once again, then, we see that there is a doubleness to language, especially literary language. I think of it as metaphor with an emphasis not on sameness but on difference. We could call it the polysemous quality of the word. Silence is in the word, and the strangeness is there, too, as long as we don't try to grasp it (which can lead only to death).

Bob

# 10. Wrestling with *Ulysses, Oedipus Rex,* and *Hamlet*

Bob,

Surely our unique pain is on a par with our unique pleasure or our unique doubt or our unique conviction. Are we by nature isolated with these things, unable to speak of them except through effort and risk, that of a skater alone out on a lake with ever-thinning ice?

And a poet—why does one person roll the dice on striving for that role, when nothing in the world suggests, much less assures, that that voice will attain coherence (or forge a new noncoherence), or will even break silence and absorb the cost, with Beckett, to "fail, fail again, fail better"?

Is it will or stubbornness? Fear of silence or love of Whitman's "valved voice"? And speaking, as you did, of language as polysemous, I am just now wrestling with Joyce's *Ulysses.* So much of the writing feels forced, an ego having something to prove rather than a fully authentic work of art seeking to express a soul and / or nurture another. Or was that kind of authenticity far from his intent? I won't make that judgment. But is all art on a continuum somewhere between the two poles of utter self-glorification and selfless expression benefiting the reader / viewer / listener? Where would Dante, Beethoven, and Van Gogh fall on that continuum?

Art and ego: twin poles of self-glorification and selflessness

Regarding our area: language. I'll risk continuing the poem that started in upstate New York, all the way back in my first letter to you, with a "return to music by the pool":

But the music—where is it? Light made rhythmic,
freed from the eye, what does it care for
the sun or water kissing concrete?

Strung sound lodged between brain and inner ear,
hungry to return like Carolina wrens to the Hudson Valley
where new nests evoke previous nests, new eggs
evoke forgotten eggs, long disintegrated after new life
cracked them open from within.

Just here, the word "evoke" sticks with me, resonates beyond the poem's use, and I search memory (apologies to Blake) to find that in *The Risk of Reading* you discuss the value of linguistic narrative vs. electronic images, and I land on this iamb by way of the psychoanalyst Jacques Lacan: "Language is not to inform, but evoke." Evoke: to summon or recall to the conscious mind. Not to discover, or to settle for, or even to remember, but to *summon*, to recall. I summon that which I need, and I recall that which had meaning. Summon from where, then? For the religious, perhaps from a deity. For others, from the unconscious mind.

Blake eschews memory, reminding us that to summon is not to remember, but to create. As if we know what we need but can't put our finger on it because it hasn't consciously existed yet. All we have is its vague outline, or unheard notes, or scent. No, not Proust's scent of the madeleine recalling what he had already known, but rather, for us, for the visitor at the pool, something new—music not yet heard, yet urgently needed if we are to be whole.

In *The Risk of Reading*, you give us Lacan: "It is through the rich texture of language . . . that we have the best chance of finding what we seek: the response of the other whom we have questioned in order to find out something about ourselves."

And revisiting your very early gambit to me, where you lay out some broad topics in your notebooks, there's language and literature in relation to the sublime; to the ethical imagination; to the ineffable; to silence.

We have explored silence, and thought about the act of writing as a rebellion against it. But what of the ineffable? Surely this is a concept at odds with our rational age—one conceived, I'd think, in the preclassical mind, when mystery not only held sway, but was revered, at the center of the tribe's life.

Consider the Oracle of Delphi, where the priestess spoke from deep under the domed rock, usually in riddles. Was she up against the ineffable? I have to think so. People came to hear her put into language that which, ironically, can't be spoken: a riddle or conundrum that might lead to a truth *for that listener only*. A listener now in the throes of discovery, receiving a summoned or evoked message of wholly personal meaning. The listener comes to know that within himself which can lead him to the truth; and it comes in relationship to another—the priestess who leads him to himself.

A truth summoned for an audience of one

Let's remember Oedipus in this regard. The Oracle spoke to him not in a riddle, but plainly: "You will kill your father and have children with your mother." For Oedipus, this was no doubt easily dismissed as a false positive, until he saw it come true—a prediction that, because of his ignorance about himself, could in no way have swayed his action. His self-knowledge came too late. The truth was nowhere in him.

Centuries later, Shakespeare has Hamlet see his deceased father in his mind's eye. A visual manifestation of the ineffable? Or a kind of personal oracle ("Oh my prophetic soul")? Why not both? Side note: This in a character who is one of the great talkers! Does Hamlet's verbosity hide his fear that he won't, or can't, capture truth in language? That, indeed, "the rest is silence"?

David

# 11. Where Did the Music Come From?

David,

It just struck me that your insights into the distinction between "inform" and "evoke," the lessons of prophecy drawn from the Oracle at Delphi, and your new lines of verse resonating with the music of poetic wonder near the end of your recent comments, all summon me to a poem you wrote long ago—"Graveside"—a poem that still lives today in the poetry pamphlet, *Echo Aonides*, that we created at Brown. I quote only a couple of lines here as a remembrance today:

> And after the music we loved, Lord how we loved.
> And the victory is that it is. In spite of all our love
> it simply is.
> It is and it has no memory.

Now, as I asked before in a different context, where did that music come from? Why is it evoked at that moment in the language of the poem? And who else at such a young age could call up in his listener the being and nonbeing, the singularity of the timeless grave? I remain speechless.

Bob

# 12. Doors Open

Bob,

As always, you've got me thinking, and I took a look at the poem "Graveside." Music does appear kind of naturally, doesn't it? A quick answer might be that, of course, an evening like that had to involve music. Sixties pop / rock or something deeper—classical or baroque, Bob Dylan or Vivaldi.

At the same time, could Erato, muse of lyric poetry, have been hovering along with her sisters Euterpe and Polymnia, the one for singing, the one for hymning? I'll posit that they were both present for that evening of music and love, and for the writing of the poem, recalled later in tranquility.

I find the line "It [the grave] is and it has no memory" terribly haunting, in that, for the speaker. the grave eradicates not just life, but the muses' mother, and therefore them—leading I'm sure to his bitter tongue in the penultimate line.

This anticipates the line on the back cover of *Echo Aonides* where we have St. Augustine ruminating on the cost of the muses' demise—spirits fall, civilization falls. Where in me did all that arise? I like to think that, as with you, in embracing poetry at a young age I opened the doors to it all, and chose never to close them.

David

# 13. Black Fire / White Fire

David,

W hile walking slowly, I took an uncharted path and seem to have wound up somewhere else. In the meantime, perhaps you will find this passage from Roberto Calasso in his *Book of All Books* worthy of thought?

> It was because the Torah was written with black fire on white fire that it could be read in two contrasting ways—either as an uninterrupted text, not divided into words or in the traditional fashion, a sequence of stories and precepts. Read the first way, the uninterrupted text became a list of names. Stories and precepts melted away, as if by fire. But some Cabalists in Gerona went further. Why insist on a plurality of names? The whole Torah should be read as a single name. The Name of the Holy One. Azriel even said that Genesis 36, which lists the descendants of Esau and is generally thought an unimportant passage, should not be considered as fundamentally distinct from the Ten Commandments. They were part of the same structure and all equally necessary.

What do you think?

Bob

# 14. Quick Confession

Bob,

I 'll confess that I don't follow the passage from Calasso—or at least its significance for us. Can you share your thoughts on it?

David

# 15. Do I Wake or Sleep?

David,

Take my last as just another detour; no reason to follow it, unless you desire to. I was thinking, in part, about that music that the eye cannot see. It is like the ripples of water in a dream (or in your poem), the ripples of rhythm that fade in and out, fold into each other, flow not as sight but as vision. I was also struck by how we can be summoned (not "informed"), depending on how we approach what is in front of us (the text, the music, and so on).

Let me try to explain.

The original Hebrew scrolls had no vowels and no spaces between words—so we might say they provided something like a dream text. It flowed endlessly, but the reader had very difficult work ahead. The reader provided the vowels and decided where one word ended and another began—so in one sense, he helped to create the text (he dreamt with the text). To make matters even more difficult, everything, even the smallest mark on the page, the most minor character in the story, the most easily overlooked gesture, were all to be considered of equal importance.

How does this relate to us, today? We are summoned by the music; we are summoned by the dream text. Are we summoned by poetry?

The dream text is made of fire, in part, because it is a self-consuming artifact (as the literary critic Stanley Fish might say), a burnt book that can only exist when we, as if in a dream, are summoned by it. One way of reading is to read for the story and the

The reader is summoned by the dream text of the poem

49

precepts—the way most of us read most of the time today. But this is not the only way to read.

It was something like that that I was thinking about when I sent you the Calasso passage. Of course, I was also thinking about your sun and the stars created at the beginning. I like to believe that we cannot see the stars during the day because the light of the sun blinds us to them. Yet, at night, with the background of darkness, the stars are radiant and illuminated, a vast multitude. So here too there are contrasting readings. Black fire on white fire. Is it the dreams of night that bring us to the light of dawn, or is it the light of day that hides the illumination that only the darkness can bring forth? Some Kabbalists say that the letters fly up above the scrolls when they are on fire. Fire cannot consume itself. And perhaps music too? Keats demanded, we call the "soft pipes" to play "Not to the sensual ear, but, more endear'd / Pipe to the spirit ditties of no tone."

Do I wake or sleep?

Changing focus, I now find that your verse—starting with "But the music—where is it?"—right to the end, evokes the equivalent of what Keats must have meant when he was dreaming of the kind of poetry that was still yet to be achieved, the poetry of "the finer tone" as he called it. Music overflowing with beauty and truth, not recollected, not known before, but created for the first time, summoned from what you call the "long-gone eggs" perhaps. It all seems exactly right: "light made rhythmic, freed from the eye"— not the visible, but sound, the rich texture of the language of the stranger, the response of the other (including the stranger in ourself).

But, as you ask, is all this writing primarily for self-glorification (ego, narcissism, sovereignty, kingship, pride), or is it primarily an attempt at selfless expression, a gesture of empathy and compassion, a kind of sacrifice?

Let me add a related question: Is writing an act of violence, a disruption (if not a killing), or is it an act of protection, a covering for the terror that lurks just beneath the surface? Does writing then allow us to open and challenge what otherwise seems necessary, or rather does it provide a husk, a way of covering and closing off the core below—a protection, in other words, a kind of generous lie in opposition to the swirling void or terrifying voice at the core? The vocable perhaps being the distraction, but perhaps within it also a sign of the truth we might find at its edge, the silence just hidden at the margins.

If writing is a rebellion against the silence, as you have said, we need also ask, What about the ineffable—the riddle we yearn to solve, the question that we cannot fully answer—the gap between our human imperfection and a divine perfection, men and the gods, the written world and the unwritten world? Surely writing provides readers with a form of hope—the possibility of living in the "in-between," in the gap that otherwise would drive us on or defeat us.

Literature provides us with the hope of living in the gap between human imperfection and divine perfection

Is writing a struggle between living and dying, eros and thanatos oscillating within us and around us? Is our death the one universal natural fact that cannot be voiced, while human language provides us hope and keeps us alive?

You mention the Oracle at Delphi, her prophecies and her riddles. I would say that all important literature, poetry and prose fiction alike, is made up of riddles, not answers but questions. In fact, every word contains a question within it. Each word struggles against itself. And each word struggles for a connection with all the other words in the world that surrounds it.

I would agree with you when you say that the oracle offers "a truth for that listener only." For me, this is very much like saying that we all read the same book (novel, short story, poem), but we each read it differently. This is perhaps what Kafka, too, had in mind in his scene in the section called "Before the Law" in *The Trial.* A "man from the country" sits each day in a chair before the door of the law but never enters. On the last day before his death, too late, he is told that the door was always open to him—that it was, in fact, created for him alone, but he never entered.

Same with some of the Talmudist commentators who say that when the Ten Commandments were revealed to the thousands of Israelites at the bottom of Mt Sinai, and they heard that there was only one God, they all agreed, but each one assumed a different version of this one God, a personal God. So, I say, same book, but a different reading each time. In the Jewish tradition, not a single word in the Hebrew Bible, from Genesis to Chronicles, can be changed. But there is an infinite number of interpretations, all acceptable but incomplete, unique paths for careful and responsible consideration.

You offer a wonderful image—the writer like "a skater on a lake with ever-thinning ice." Perhaps we write against that inevitability. But I think it's the pain as much as the pleasure, the trauma as much as the joy, that keeps writers writing. It's the attempt at the impossible, the desire to give voice to the pain, the insistence on refusing to be defeated by the trauma but not being able to represent clearly the pain, not being able to give form to the trauma (or the terror) that is often the struggle of the writer. It is what summons the courage of the writer. It is part of his sacrifice. Is this a kind of silence that intensifies as we skate closer to the edge of that ever-thinning ice? Is this an example of the writer struggling to speak the ineffable? "Fail, fail again, fail better." Can we call Beckett's saying a statement about disappearance?

We might want to distinguish knowing from creating. We cannot know the ineffable, any more than we can know "the core," or the truth (be it God or terror), the essence of things (or the Thing), but we can create novels, poems, art, and so on to remind us of our human connectivity. Blake thought creation was the Fall. Yet it helps keep us human and alive, though many writers today seem to think that writing (art in general) is a fiction (a lie or a ruse).

Called to create— despite our lack of ultimate knowledge

It may be that our job is to create even if we cannot ultimately know. That is, we question, and so even if we are destroyed, we are not defeated (as Hemingway said). We continue on. We imitate God (His creation), though we do not know Him. This too is part of the riddle of the ineffable.

You mention Oedipus and Hamlet. Oedipus is a poor reader, as you suggest. He cannot find his story—until it is much too late—in the story he hears. No self-reflection. Perhaps a nod, though, to the sense that with blindness comes insight. Perhaps on the other side of blindness, the other side of trauma, insight arrives.

One problem with Oedipus is that he cannot "create" his own story, he cannot rebel against the necessity of the given. By contrast, Hamlet, in great pain and deeply depressed, riddled by a ghost, does finally create his own story, and it is a story within a story, a play within a play, a nod to self-reflection and recognition, that wins out. Coleridge thought Hamlet was too abstract and

contemplative, but he clearly saw him as one of the great characters in all literature. To me, Hamlet (the great talker, as you indicate) leaves much to silence, but he is closer than Oedipus to the
Oracle at Delphi. He gives us a riddle because, in the end, he is in
touch with himself in a way that Oedipus could not be. Hamlet is
the riddle that he creates for himself and for us.

Which takes me back to those "long-gone eggs" that you
evoked earlier on. This, too, is a riddle to me. Are these eggs the
original eggs from time immemorial, or are they just copies?—not
the original name, the name that cannot be named, but a copy of
that name, a substitution for the original, a deception (like a play
within a play), a fiction that we nevertheless need to keep our humanity?

It may very well all be a fiction, but, if so, we are fortunate to
have it.

Bob

# 16. What Is Hope?

Bob,

A while back, you asked, "Is writing an act of violence, a disruption (if not a killing), or is it an act of protection, a covering for the terror that lurks just beneath the cover?"

We're up on the California coast, at a place called Sea Ranch, a community built on coastal cliffs with views of exotic rock formations, inaccessible coves, and cypress trees growing nearly horizontal due to wind.

It couldn't be more different from your terrain, Dartmouth and New Bedford. Yet that very terrain and seascape actually looms large at this moment. The house we've rented is spacious, with huge windows looking at the Pacific. The owners collect books and art, and on the nightstand is an impressive paper edition of *Moby-Dick* (Penguin, 2001) with an introduction by Nathaniel Philbrick, which I dipped into last night. Philbrick mentions Chapter 14, "Nantucket," as being his favorite, with Melville's writing at its best.

And of this writing? Does it shed light on our discussion? It is expository, yet underpinned by a specific kind of truth germane to prose fiction: its premise invites the reader to pretend that it is portraying reality as a photograph might, bringing before the mind's eye a scene from nature—in this case, a small island off of Massachusetts, a fictional Nantucket, steeped in the whaling trade. But is Melville's portrait accurate, even realistic? Or rather, is it an imaginative leap via the eyes and sensibility, not of Melville directly, but of his character, Ishmael? It's not a Nantucket I've ever seen, but desolate, a spit of sand, inhabited barely if at all.

Through Ishmael, Melville is, in the months of composing his novel, imagining a world where final truth will reside in the form of a great white whale of the imagination, endowed with malevolence. It's a worthy object of hatred—indeed, one despised by the autocrat Ahab, who also never existed, but who, by his (and Melville's) dark obsession, brought his ship to ruin, killing all but one of his crew.

As for Nantucket itself, Philbrick points out something interesting—that Melville himself never visited the island until after *Moby-Dick* was published. (Hence his need to fictionalize it?) So really, what is Melville creating? An island of the mind, just as the whale is an evil force of the mind. He's using narrative prose in the service of myth and more, as the vehicle of his own dark dreams. Didn't Coleridge do the same in *Rime of the Ancient Mariner?* And Sophocles in the *Oedipus* trilogy? And Shakespeare in *Hamlet?* (Rhodri Lewis's new book is reputedly opening up this aspect of the play.)

Each of these writers chose to break silence, or was driven to do so, as "an act of protection, a covering for the terror that lurks just beneath the cover." The terror just beneath the surface of all these journeys. Evil whale; dark fate-and-death-delivering albatross; Oedipus's encounter with the hateful self; Hamlet's trajectory toward revenge and death.

Yet what of hope? That without which we cannot live? In each case, the writer chooses to unmask the terror of life, so we see it face to face. Yet in each case something else lies embedded; the act of writing asserts that language and voice are choices preferable to silence. Why? To show hope. *Moby-Dick* ends with Ishmael surviving to tell us the tale, exactly as the Ancient Mariner tells the wedding guest not merely the cautionary tale of his killing of the albatross, with death and desolation following, but the tale of his redemption and survival (as a result of his blessing of the only life left on the ship—the snakes slithering in the sea beside the ship). As for Oedipus, his daughters live on in *Oedipus at Colonus,* and in *Hamlet,* order, and the state, are salvaged to live on too. And so hope is reborn.

*Literature gives us hope in the face of life's terror*

None of these tales dares to end in total death and desolation. The same is true of *The Odyssey, The Divine Comedy, King Lear, Paradise Lost,* and "The Wasteland." In all these works, writers skate out to the furthest reaches of the spirit, the thinnest ice, but make it back to us.

I'm recalling Joseph Campbell's *Hero with a Thousand Faces,* where the common archetype of any hero's journey is the return with some hard-won truth that nourishes and sustains the tribe.

So yes, as you say, "perhaps writing provides readers with that hope—the possibility of living in the 'in-between.' "

In this context, I offer Paul Celan's haunting lines:

> The carving of the crow
> Like chalk screeching
> On dirt or board
> Makes legible the sign
> Of the liminal
> The sojourner
> At the boundary of barbed wire
> On the fringe of the unwritten:
> Marks of courage there
> Traces of the quest
> Bringing the new
> Back home.

The written versus the unwritten. In the written: trial, thin ice, and eventual hope. And the unwritten? The void and nothingness. If our theme is the courage of breaking silence, then it's also the courage of hope, and the huge risk it takes to find it.

David

# 17. Events of Disruption, Events of Promise

David,

V isiting again the issue of silence. This theme is inspiring to me, in a multitude of registers. In fact, I want to tell you now more about the last few years of my life with cancer and what, in particular, it has meant in terms of my thinking about literature and language and its connection to my heritage—Judaism. Threaded within my comments throughout our thoughtful exchanges so far, I have left fragments and traces of this kind of context, and I'd like to expand on them now. I hope that what I share here is also related to what we can and cannot know, what we write and refrain from writing. It will take me a while to explain, so please excuse me for that. I suppose I am pursuing what I want to know—which is precisely what I cannot know.

When I retired from UMass Dartmouth after a long career as an English professor, I realized, perhaps for the first time, that I knew nothing. The retirement was accompanied with a diagnosis of stage 4 pancreatic cancer and a framed certificate announcing my new status as professor emeritus. I put the certificate in my closet and wondered why I had never known that stages 1-3 had apparently passed unnoticed through my body. Only a CAT scan followed by a biopsy and the examination of cells under a microscope made the invisible visible, gave a voice to silence. Only then could we get a diagnosis and a name.

It was the voice of the oncologist that made it official for me. Stages 1-3, never seen, were now all but forgotten. The CAT scan on the computer screen illuminated the disease and made the situation clear: I had become a professor emeritus with stage 4 pancreatic cancer, a man with chaos in his body, cancer that had spread from the pancreas to the liver. It was time to put my house in order: "Prepare for the worst, hope for the best," as the doctor said.

A week later, that same voice resonated with good news. My cancer was a rare type, only four percent of pancreatic cancer patients had it—neuroendocrine pancreatic cancer. There was no cure, but it offered the gift of time. Steve Jobs and Aretha Franklin each lived for several years with the same diagnosis. Although one website did claim that only about one percent of people diagnosed lived for more than five or six years, that was not an unreasonable hope for me at the time. I went forth, dancing.

I had experienced previous disruptions. My oldest son Jonathan had died from the terrible disease of heroin addiction on August 20, 1995, twenty years before. An event inscribed in my heart now and forever, carried with me each day.

My younger son Jeremy had suffered a mysterious spinal trauma a few years later after a trip to Brazil. Temporarily paralyzed, warned that he might never walk again, he was truly fortunate. With the patience of a humble warrior, he called up all the desire he could muster and the insatiable will to walk again—and he did walk, developing into a superb defense attorney for justice, fighting not for "what is" but for "what ought to be." To me, he honors the possibilities of a vision burnt into his heart through the passion he shares with his brother now and forever.

And my wife Linda knows the anguish of disruption, as well, from the earliest years of our marriage, when an inscrutable and undefined growth in her upper jaw and gums demanded several painful surgeries in New York and again in Boston before she regained some semblance of reasonable relief. I could not live without her patience and care now.

I mention these events of disruption because I trust they were destined to happen. Paradoxically, I also believe that they were not planned, they could have been otherwise, they were contingent and random, without foundation. They were created out of nothing, an unexplained silence, perhaps a whisper that cannot be explained. In each case, it was a silence which shook our small world.

Destined, yet random and inexplicable

Such events help to provide a context for my thinking throughout our discussions, my friend David, thinking which emerges from such disruptions—a response to a call to go forth, to carry on, to turn toward a belief that what seems impossible is possible, what is not seen can be seen . . . but not yet.

Or, to put it the other way around, my responses often seem to come from a disruption, a call, beginning as a silence which came when it came, then erupted into a thunderous voice. Our wonderful dialogue, for me today, works within that gap.

I want to put it this way right now. You might read the following as a kind of stutter (or perhaps a ramble . . . ).

"At the beginning"—or "In the beginning"—or "With the beginning"—it was as if there was a call to me, and then a turning away from nothing, a turning toward a beginning. It was as if I could barely hear a whisper, a silence spinning in the world. But it was a silence with a voice of thunder, as well: a call demanding a response. It remains an unexplained event that I would eventually imagine as a dream place, an in-between place, or, at times, following the language of the philosopher Maurice Blanchot or the poet Edmond Jabès, I might name it "no place." But it is not an empty place—that I know. The world in ongoing communion with another.

Thank goodness, you, my old and dear friend, David Beckman, met me at the threshold. It can happen in less than a second, in a single breath, a surprise sometimes without disturbance. "Hello, I must be going," Groucho Marx sings in one of his Marx Brothers movies. I'd bet he is thinking about the polysemous language of Hebrew then—the word "shalom," which means "hello" and "good-bye," and "peace." Spin it like a dreidel, dig into it— Marx knows we are all coming and going, and hoping for peace.

At least two are required to create time, though, and so dialogue, the rhythm and responsibility of responding to the call from the other, together with the demand to pay close attention

The dialogue of literature— a way of creating time through the connection between two humans to the polysemous and multidimensional language within the world itself, remained intensely interesting for me.

So through the process of naming (call it *diagnosis* if you prefer) there also came an acknowledgment that dialogue could become a way of creating time, a way of walking through language.

I was no longer pursuing the stability of the truth as some kind of universal and abstract proposition, but rather as a poetic wonder, a particular amazement of each precious and unique life. It was as if I was on a quest now for the language of a shooting star or of the blinking moment between sleeping and waking, or the instant just before the break of dawn.

It is now as if reading and writing, the call and response, the silence and the voice—all became part of the flow and wonder of the dream place, not eternal but infinite, not closed but open, ongoing.

To me, reading and dreaming are attuned to each other in this way. Both are events with a promise, flowing as they go forth. At times, I sense a temporary resistance as I go, a pause to consider, to find my breath, but there is always an insistence to keep the dialogue moving, between me and my friend or even a stranger before me. It is as if I live within all the language of the world that surrounds me, the language that I now owe a debt to. I am reminded of the words of Sven Birkerts in his *Gutenberg Galaxy*:

> Reading, because we control it, is adaptable to our needs and rhythms. We are free to indulge our subjective associative powers. We just don't read the words, we dream our lives in their vicinity.

How else can I put this? For me, language, especially literary language, carries a double negation. an endless creation and decreation. It offers a way to glimpse what has not yet been seen, and at the same time it questions what we see, what we think we know. It is always messy, like life itself. Without it, each unique and precious life would surely collapse.

I have learned that it is an inconvenience to live with stage 4 cancer, to know that the sickness unto death has no cure. It might get me down, might make it difficult at times to stand upright. But everyone struggles with a similar dilemma. That dilemma is mortal life itself. Thank you for the gift of friendship and for all the gifts that accompany it: the imagination and remembrance, language and time, the encounter with the other who infinitely calls for a response, the other who opens possibilities through a demand to pay close attention, to listen and to act through the language of what is and what ought to be.

At its best, literary language always carries with it traces of this doubleness. It works as if in a gap between the speaker and the listener, between what is familiar and what is strange, what is and what ought to be. As the poet Jabès claims, it keeps open the on-going quest "to unfold the endless space of the question." I take that sense of "endless space" as the equivalent of my dream place now, an unexplained place where language is not simply a tool for instrumental use, a means to an end, but rather a movement through time, tracing a possible path to life as it can be, a glimpse of something else.

The endless space of the question

Long ago, the philosopher Walter Benjamin suggested something similar: it is not news that we need, but stories that grow in the reader through time. The reader interprets and translates the original story that always says more than it knows. The story questions us as we question the story. This is life itself in all its wonder and surprise, an "infinite conversation" (to borrow the title of one of Maurice Blanchot's many books). It is not idle chatter, however, but for me, communion or a covenant created in-between at least two of us. If you prefer, we can call it a story.

Once upon a time, I cofounded an alternative sentencing program for convicted criminals and named it Changing Lives Through Literature. And once upon a time I cofounded and named the Center for Jewish Culture on the UMass Dartmouth campus. There are probably written records that such moments happened, but for me now they exist primarily as stories wandering through the imagined flow of time, through remembrance and imagination. They mingle today with the inconvenience of an incurable cancer and the intense desire to carry on. Eros and thanatos in dialogue, I imagine—the experience of finite life.

In the midst of all this, I began to read with a rejuvenated fervor. Not about cancer, but about language and literature, friendship and Judaism.

How little I knew about Judaism. I reread passages from the Hebrew Bible, engaged in dialogue about the Zohar with my brother, studied the history and philosophy of Hellenism and the time around the beginning of Christianity. And in the midst of this journey, I recalled an early Sunday afternoon fifty-six years ago, strolling through Hyde Park in London with my new bride Linda on our honeymoon. We stopped at the famous Speaker's Corner that bright Sunday to listen to a young man's complaint. He must be crazed, we assumed—wildly shouting out some nonsense about how Jews should not consider themselves part of the Western white world rooted in Greco-Roman Christianity. Jews, he claimed, are people of color (as he was), wanderers on this Earth.

A crazy voice—never to be forgotten

Why I remember that so vividly remains a question for me. It is a voice mixed with all the other voices I hear now as I continue to read and write and dream. Perhaps that voice was not the mere babble of idle chatter, but a voice speaking to me about my own unique destiny? Like the touch of a book in the local library so many years ago. Is it possible?

But now I am not there. I am aimlessly pacing back and forth at home in my study. I pause at my bookshelves. There are hundreds of books here, without order or logical arrangement. The shelves cover about half of the four walls, a large room painted sky blue, which Linda designed. Out of the corner of my eye, I glimpse a book by the philosopher André Neher called *The Exile of the Word*.

I cannot be certain—perhaps the book is looking at me?

Bending forward, I open to a passage from Neher's book: "Judaism does not know, and it rejects, the Greco-Latin cleavage, re-adopted by Christianity, and this rejection is symbolized in the history of a word." Neher is not talking about the Greek word *logos*. He is talking about the Hebrew word, *davar*. Am I dreaming?

I turn to another passage, this one about the biblical Abraham: "Abraham was the inventor of the word," it says. But it is not God's Word that Neher is talking about, but an echo of that Word, "the human word": the creative word connected to time and history, to dialogue and translation. Abraham breathed new life into the exiled word, it might be said, preserving traces of *davar* through dialogue and through human history and time.

62

What does the Hebrew Bible suggest about Abraham? What about commentary from the Zohar? How about the ancient legends about such a man? I need to pursue this. I am not primarily interested in discovering a theme or getting a picture of the situation, nor am I focused on being informed about some abstract cause / effect sequence of events which might appear logical or graspable. What I want now is to trace the flow of the language opening to me, follow traces left from the disruption and atrocity of the Tower of Babel through the imagined journey of Abraham himself. "Abraham was the inventor of the word"? I wonder.

Near his death, Kafka became interested in the story of the Tower of Babel. He questioned the stability of the tower's foundation. He thought that perhaps burrowing down into the ground rather than trying to rise up to heaven might have worked better. Based on one of his last stories, "The Burrow," he seems to have finally concluded that, either way, human beings were in for it.

In a late letter to his doctor-friend Klopstock, though, Kafka suggested that the tower episode might not have ended in disruption if the people had built it only halfway to heaven. I doubt such a solution would have satisfied Kafka. Like Kafka, I want to know more than I can know for certain.

Neher suggests that the hunter Nimrod—let's call him the CEO of the Babel project—set himself against the flow of God's Word. It is as if the tower is a big business operation, and mostly committee work. Totalitarian and closed-off, basically an abstraction. The builders do not speak on their own behalf; their words are spoken for them and then recycled to become repetitive news, instrumental and dehumanized. Perhaps it was somewhat like the use of talking points on Fox News or CNN?

The inhuman language of the builders of the Tower of Babel

Like the whole systematic and technical project, the language of the builders has become an abstraction, a brick or stone, a commodity—just like the builders themselves and their useless work. The flow of words has become a thing without uniqueness, without breath, without sound and rhythm: a stream of tools for measurement in terms of quantity and sale.

Somewhere there is a midrash from a medieval rabbi on this. Apparently, the builders mourned deeply whenever a brick was broken. But when a man, or even a baby, fell from the tower, no one noticed, much less shed a tear.

Under such conditions, God could have done otherwise, I assume. He could have given up on language, abandoned His creation. Instead, In His compassion, he offers His creatures another chance. He creates Babel, the beginning of human language and translation, a dream place for time and dialogue, an alternative way through Abraham to stand against the nonsense of the builders, to turn away from the ideology that drives the builders to use brick and stone to fashion a name for themselves in an attempt to become idols and celebrities for worship. If the original *davar* has been disrupted, so too has the world now in need of repair. Fragments of *davar*, call them sparks of light if you will, remain for those willing to turn towards them, work with them for the benefit of humankind.

And then emerges Abraham, born Abram, the inventor of the human word, the language that becomes, in the midst of Babel, the creative flow of human dialogue and human history. He is the unique Abraham, irreplaceable, the one who helps to create, as Neher and others agree, the first challenging dialogue between man and the transcendent God (the vertical dialogue for human justice in Sodom) and the first genuine interhuman dialogue in finite history (the horizontal dialogue between him and his wife Sarah)—a type of I-Thou dialogue which people like Martin Buber and Emmanuel Levinas must have noted much later with admiration.

Unlike earlier dialogues between Adam and Eve or Eve and the snake, or the one that should have taken place between Cain and Abel, these new challenging dialogues leave space for the other. They are responsible and filled with respect in their exchanges, lacking excuses and lies and erroneous belief. It is as if the I has turned to the Thou, and the word in exile through genuine dialogue can carry a creative force in-between them. Can we call that "creative force in-between" a glimpse of "something else" in the gap?

Abram becomes Abraham as two letters are added through the flow of the process of naming. It is a crossing-over, a kind of translation, a way of reaching the far side of the Jordan River. To me, it is a way of reading and rereading, of stumbling across the border of an enclosed egoism to turn toward another, to speak and listen to each other, an expansion of what is to be glimpsed, a promise of what is and what is not yet.

*Bereshit bara Elohim.* Those are the words that begin the Hebrew Bible. Black marks on white parchment, they are written for finite mortal readers. They twist and turn within their own unique silence, ever open to question and interpretation. They are multidimensional, polysemous, inviting new relations and infinite possibilities. They discourage dogma, prefer *aggadah* (stories) to *halakkah* (the law), as Abraham Heschel suggests. Turn them and turn them, and you will find everything there. William Blake said something apt in this regard: you can find the world in a grain of sand. One law for the ox and the wolf makes no sense.

So, I like to dream that God gave Abraham another gift of human language, a gift of traces of *davar*, scattered fragments with sparks of possibility for those willing to commit themselves to justice and the compassionate work ahead.

The first letter of the Hebrew alphabet, which many scholars now argue preceded the Greek, is *aleph*. But the first letter of the Hebrew Bible is *bet* (B). *Bereshit*. Why?

As I tried to indicate earlier, there is no end to this beginning. Nor is there an end of interpretation to the next two-word phrase: *bara Elohim* ("created Elohim," or is it "Elohim created" or . . . ?). If we imagine, as Neher has suggested, that genuine interactive dialogue and human language start through Abraham, questions and interpretation become an important part of the work of human life.

For example, what do these opening words of the Hebrew Bible suggest? Elohim created with the beginning? Elohim created in the beginning? Elohim created at the beginning? Elohim created out of nothing? Did something else create Elohim? Was this creation the making of the world through language? Was the word God and also with God (as the Gospel of John interprets it)? Was this creation a thunderous voice that was the beginning of separation, an original disruption? That is two *bet*—*Bereshit bara* and a silent *aleph* that precedes *bet* in the Hebrew alphabet. Is the phrase *bara Elohim* best considered as the voice of a call that opens for the reader to enter and take action?

Here, then, I would suggest, is not the word as *logos* but the word as *davar*. Let me further explain. It is not the use of language

The word as *davar*: poetry, not philosophy

as a sign pointing to something else, but language itself inviting the reader to enter into it. As Neher and others suggest, it is not Greek, with its cause / effect reasoning and its determined attempt to gather together a complete and ordered world for contemplation at an illusory distance; rather it is Hebrew, with its personal and existential twists and turns, its knotting and unknotting, its rhythm and indetermined flow. It is an attempt to keep open an incomplete path for further possibilities. It is poetry, not philosophy. It does not offer answers, but questions.

According to rabbinic commentators, Abraham turns away from his father's idolatry and the idolatry of the builders of the tower, becomes the unique human being, creating the creation of human language at the beginning of history and dialogue as we imagine it. We might even say that language creates Abraham, just as he creates human language. It is a story about Abraham and a story about human language, a story about turning toward something else, a leaving and a going forth: Indeed, "changing your life," as Rilke advises in his "Archaic Torso of Apollo."

Of course, David, we might agree that it didn't really happen. But we continue to talk about it anyway. It is not a recollection of facts, not news or mundane history. It is remembrance: in Hebrew, *zakhor*. The Talmud says that even if there is no evidence, you can't absolutely conclude an event didn't happen. Maurice Blanchot says Abraham is "the wandering word" of finite time, very much like the vulnerable and ever-questioning words of all significant literature (I would say): infinitely indeterminate, infinitely ambivalent and paradoxical. Turning away from the closed brick of abstraction and inevitable commodification, Abraham turns toward the wonder of the particular and existential, the multidimensional call of language, the event of words in motion. It is the gift of language as we might know it; not fallen language, but language in the gap, open now and forever through time for endless interpretation and infinite possibilities. Much can be glimpsed in that language, in its silence and in its voice, in its call and in its response. It is the work of each unique and precious person to enter deeply into it in his or her relation to the other. It connotes dialogue. And it calls for "true friendship," David—like ours through the language we share.

Language in the gap, with its endless possibilities

For me, this is also a way of reading now. Picking up a book lying on a shelf, committing myself to it, listening to its call, keeping myself and the book alive by paying close attention to it, responding to its flow of language as I go. It is an invitation, an opening that drives me onwards. Always a discussion. Always an act of love spinning through time.

There are other stories about Abraham. Certainly, they never happened. Legends about his refusal to accompany the angel of death when his time had expired, his destiny fulfilled. Some say a miracle happened then. God relented for a while, called the angel back, gave Abraham additional time. It didn't happen. But when I think about Steve Jobs or Aretha Franklin or all those who died too soon from pancreatic cancer after their diagnosis, I believe that I, too, am living within a kind of miracle, especially if we think of a miracle as an unexplained time beyond most statistics of medical reasoning, and other signs of abstract bricks and stones.

There is more in the world than we can see, and I am convinced that the honest engagement with literature awakens us to this possibility. Through the feverish and intense reading that I have done over the last few years, I am beginning to lean towards the voice I heard in Hyde Park over half a century ago. Not the intent of the speaker that day, but his inside story, the difference between Greek and Hebrew (as I have dreamt it), between *logos* and *davar*, between the Judaism that I have created in my own dream place and the powerful establishment of what is conventionally referred to today as the mainstream Western civilization. I do not mean to imply that it is incorrect to think about a Judeo-Christian tradition, or that Jews should be considered, as critic Geoffrey Hartman has suggested, an important "third pillar" in the West, or that Jews have not made major contributions to Western thinking and the Western way of life. Of course, they have. But it is also clear that the history of the West is often a history of anti-Judaism, a history of difference and a suffering because of that difference. Too often, the Jews have been seen only as the other, a stubborn stumbling block, a problem that needs a violent and final solution.

So permit me now to change the angle of our dialogue for a brief final thought about the issue of silence in the context of poetic language. It brings us all the way back to our early discussion of Adorno, who first claimed it was a scandal to write after the Holocaust, but then seems to have changed his mind somewhat and suggested writing as an act of limited rebellion.

Three ways to respond to the horror

What are the possible ways of dealing with the horror in time, the poem as "cadaver" (as Celan puts it), the words that float up into the air as if buried in a tomb? I have heard about at least three possibilities:

1. Remain silent. Early Adorno.
2. Write it, but not say it. So it remains hidden and not misinterpreted. Somewhat like a purloined letter.
3. Write it, but then burn it before it can be read. A fire that cannot be consumed. A priceless work to be dreamed about infinitely.

But then why write? Is it a deception to confuse the reader when we know the last lamp no longer gives off light, enveloping itself in its own darkness (as Celan says)?

The Zohar says that God started to create the Hebrew alphabet in dialogue with the last letter (*tet*), which can mean "death," but then moved to the next-to-last letter (*shin*), which falls short of the end and is connected with "fire" (not "death"). Is our job to write fire until the end? Putting fire on the letters and the words. I am reminded of the Jewish sage R. Hanna ben Teradon, burned alive by the Romans for teaching Torah, who said, "The Torah is fire, and no fire can burn itself."

I also note in a recent article that the big black hole in the middle of the Milky Way has been seen much more recently by scientists. These black holes which are nothing (and perhaps the origin of everything) remind me of the gap between sounds, the white space between two words or letters, the silence which allows the absence to be present, perhaps. In neuroscience, I have recently read, there is something called the *synaptic cleft*, a space between one neuron and another. Neurons leap from one neuron to another through this synaptic cleft in order to communicate. I think that poets work in all these gaps (black holes, synaptic clefts, absences, and so on) in order to bring fire to wounded creatures like ourselves. It is risky business, but I am thankful for all such Promethean efforts. I am thankful for yours.

I am not sure you can find any fire in all of the above, but since I have been too silent before writing this last letter to you, I wanted you to know that I am still alive. And am mindful now of this passage from a Marge Piercy poem:

> We stand in the midst of the burning world
> primed to burn with compassionate love and justice
> to turn inward and find holy fire at the core
> to turn outward and see the world that is all
> of one flesh with us.

Bob

# 18. Silence Mercifully Fails, and Your Life Speaks

Bob,

I did indeed find fire, and so much more, in your last. Like seeing by way of a powerful telescope back nearly to the moment of the Big Bang, you have looked at where your life abides, and where silence yields to speech.

And, Bob, what your last letter, parts one and two, imparts to me! Your stage 4 cancer, the awful death of Jonathan, your and Linda's anguish, Jeremy's trauma and recovery to a thriving life. Events you've lived bravely through, and here you are now, having moved on to enter fully into dialogue with me.

I am humbled by your courage and strength, and avid to continue on our path together.

We have focused on writing that emerges after pain and trauma. But what of breaking silence in (or right after) joy? Who can feel joy, and stay quiet? Last night we were at a table outside a restaurant when a friend said, seemingly unprompted, "I feel happy tonight." We're not given to voicing that often. And perhaps we're even less likely to say, unprompted, "I feel unhappy tonight." Or fearful, apprehensive, nervous, confused . . . peaceful, optimistic, content. Who offers these words with any regularity? Yet their meaning is akin to the meaning of life; their utterance is what only humans can voice.

It's one thing if such speech arises from and reflects an experience in real time ("You just gave me a gift, and I feel happy"); it's quite another if it comes unprompted out of silence (the mind's black hole?).

Why do we rarely voice such basic truths unprompted? Custom? Habit? Or perhaps there is a long-standing taboo against breaking silence with unprepared-for expression. Yet don't we, in our heart of hearts, yearn for others to magically know how we feel? If someone we're close to doesn't read our thoughts (or our face or our body) and thus doesn't discern our truth, we are left with yearning.

Is it this yearning that moves us to break silence in our art, giving new meaning to "emotion recalled in tranquility"? Perhaps being driven to do so prompts us to want to write *well,* as if it's the quality of our expression that matters, not the fact of our having chosen expression to begin with.

The yearning that gives birth to art

How would Keats respond, immediately after writing "Ode on a Grecian Urn," to the idea that being possessed of yearning allowed him to craft a perfect poem? Would he prefer knowing that we are dazzled by his craft, and that we have no impulse to probe into his yearning as a separate phenomenon? (Though having just written this, I can fully imagine Keats answering, "Why not? My personal yearning is crude and temporal, where my poem is refined, fully considered, and for the ages.")

We have also posited the breaking of silence as a rebellion, and Adorno is key in this context. His suggesting that writing is, after the Holocaust, "an act of limited rebellion" is digging deep. But rebellion against what? Perhaps against his own conviction that to write is to pulverize any lingering shards of morality and decency after war's ultimate horrors, as we might feel should nuclear annihilation take out 20 cities sometime next year.

Your option #3 of possible ways to deal with "the absence"— "write it but then burn it"—is chilling. Yet burning one's early work is a time-honored recourse, particularly for maturing writers.

Have you done it? I have not. Instead, I've kept early work that I don't like or don't want seen . . . but filed it poorly, mindlessly, half-hoping it will disappear of its own volition. A coward's alternative to burning?

David

# 19. You Are What You See

David,

T he concept of burning one's early work frightens and be-
fuddles me. It strikes me as cutting off something rare and
once important, and so a violation of the self. So I now begin to
wonder about how the development of self / identity, as we conventionally understand it, and the notion of time, is in fact woven
into our discussion.

For example, the stories we create about our self which shape
the way we think about our self are often considered mental structures (the brain chattering with itself at rest) which rise to the conscious level. These are ideas (often illusions) that we might call
ego. They often block out other emotions, other creative possibilities, other temptations, and so on. They keep us within bounds,
within the rational structure of consciousness, and so supposedly
protect us within an established horizon. We might think of this
as a closed system.

When we forget to conceive of this self as a separate self, when
the ego begins to dissolve—in other words, when we lose the conscious self—we become open to a higher state (we might say), a
glimpse of open imagination beyond the horizon, even ecstasy.
We seem open to the cosmic world, connected with it, one with it.
At least, the Romantics seemed to believe this.

So people sometimes draw a distinction between alienated labor (created by clock time, separate from us) and meaningful

work (created by our human time as agents, connecting us to our body and the universe which surrounds us). Meaningful work is the fire we create with; it is neither rest nor entertainment, but it is not alienated labor, either. Its creative intensity can bring enchantment at any moment.

As I think about this, I then turn to thinking about entropy and time, although I know little about these as scientific concepts. Cognitive scientists today seem to believe that it is crucial to know how ordered or chaotic the brain is. Neurologists have suggested that predictable brain patterns, those that are organized and conventionally acceptable, produce low entropy, while randomness, wildness, and chaos create high entropy. That wildness looks dangerous, but a brain that is too efficient might become too monotonous and get stuck, lacking entropy. Being stuck is our problem today as much as randomness, probably more so. People ask,

"How do we get unstuck?" Poetry, music, meditation actually seem to quiet the rigid structures and so loosen the predetermined patterns, allowing for more entropy (chaos and randomness), an opening to renewal (joy). Many researchers have asked: is entropy a path to re-enchantment and community engagement?

These ideas resonate with and have been connected to the work of the Italian physicist Carlo Rovelli. He hints at the strong possibility that we live in a world without time. His argument is that there is no variable for time in the basic building blocks of the universe—that is, time is absent in the universe as a physical variable. Rovelli relates this to quantum gravity. In fact, he even argues that if we could film quantum events, the footage would make as much sense played backward as forward. This seems reasonable to me, although I know of no narrative that has ever been written that literally moves from the end of life to the beginning (although Fitzgerald's story "Benjamin Button" leans in that direction).

For Rovelli, the only process related to time is entropy. All events occur relative to each other, not related to any external sense of the "passing of time." For him, then, to determine whether a system really has low entropy or high entropy depends totally on a conscious observer; that is, depends on an "opinion," a totally subjective observation. So, for Rovelli, time is created by the mind. He asks, "Do we exist in time, or does time exist in us?"

74

Perhaps we can say that time is absent until we create it. A fortunate illusion—a fortunate lie, allowing us to create a story with its own truth.

Bob

# 20. Roots of Consciousness and the Self

Bob,

I very much appreciate your thoughts on self—that sometimes our ideas on it can be illusions blocking other creative possibilities. And, further, that by losing our conscious self we open the possibility of attaining a higher state and "open imagination beyond the horizon."

This is a very rich area of inquiry!

I chose to immerse myself in literature at Brown to open this possibility—to see beyond the sense of self I arrived with. Was this conscious at the time? Barely. What I did sense was that literature—the printed word—would be my doorway into some other me.

Did this require a predisposition to not accept my wholly conscious self? Yes. And additionally, a rebellion against both it and forces—social, familial, cultural—that would otherwise impel me to accept my given self and look no further?

Early on I took courage from Eliot's meditation on memory in "Rhapsody on a Windy Night":

> Whispering lunar incantations
> Dissolve the floors of memory
> And all its clear relations.

Later, I was encouraged by Proust's experience of memory, jarred open by the scallop shell of cake and revealing in his mind the vast structure of recollection. These were early enablers aiding me to open to the basement, the unconscious, in happy rebellion against the self I'd been given.

Isn't immersing oneself in a poem, almost any poem (or a great piece of prose, for that matter), a memory-dissolver, a challenge to the established self? Isn't a reader changed after absorbing Whitman, Keats, Eliot, or Proust? Yes, unless he works hard to avoid it.

I think there's another voice here—that of the will. Forgive any Nietzschean echoes, but it had to happen. What says the will to any particular self? Does it say, "Yes, I greenlight change in you." Or on the contrary, does it hit the brakes? It can do either, and in the history of a consciousness this choice may be a self-defining moment or series of moments.

Some (many?) people I encountered at Brown, and all through my life, stand out in my mind as eager to avoid embracing a changing self. The self they had was just fine, thank you very much. They were solidly who they were and wanted no change. For them, a happy coherent life required it. I hope I haven't misjudged them.

On the flip side, there were those hungry for more fundamental, risk-all change. They plunged into the realms of psychedelics or very heavy drinking. Perhaps they were true pioneers in major alternations of consciousness, or simply unthinking roll-of-the-dice funsters with self and consciousness up for grabs as part of the game.

This opens the whole topic you have so energetically immersed yourself in—the courage of reading. I obviously join you in this and am inspired by it. I just reread your essay on *Catcher in the Rye* and Holden Caulfield's journey to a better (or at least maturing) self. Now, in our dialogue, you've moved from self to brain, to Carlo Rovelli, and the concepts of entropy and timelessness, which, if I have it right, came to Rovelli under the influence of LSD. Is that testimony at odds with my earlier shelving of psychedelics as legitimate tools to surpass the given self? I must perhaps rethink.

The courage it takes to read

Then there is the issue of time you rightly invoke. Again, remaining personal, can it be that my self, expanded through the printed word, is nevertheless linear in nature and form, and therefore intimately involved with time? This feels intuitively and experientially correct, because time is a comfort to me, a touchstone for understanding, inherent in me. But are my limits brought into sharp focus when time is seen as artificial, not existing fundamentally in the universe, a creation of ours to explain our lives to ourselves? I grant that possibility.

In another life I might strive to live free from time.

There is also your inquiry about the brain being stuck, and I'm happy to get there. Surely "stuck" implies a problem, not a choice. If my will says to my self, "No, here and no further," am I stuck? I don't think so. Not any more than a car happily stored in a garage is stuck. But if my will is mute and indifferent, then I am indeed stuck.

Somehow at this point Thomas More and his reverence for self comes to mind. In *A Man for All Seasons,* playwright Robert Bolt has him say:

> When a man takes an oath, he's holding his own self in his hands, like water, and if he opens his fingers then, he needn't hope to find himself again.

What of this? Aside from the oath aspect (a whole other topic, I suppose) we do have More's conviction of self as something precious, even holy, that one betrays at one's deepest peril. I never felt this in reading—that I could open my hand and let the water of self run out—but who's to say whether it's what kept me away from psychedelics . . . that in their realm I would indeed risk too much?

Postscript: After reading your last, but before writing this, as an exercise, I substituted *convictions* for your *ideas*. Which drove me to the OED, to find, under *conviction*, six meanings. The first definition (from a 1491 legal brief under Henry VII): "the mental condition of strong belief based on satisfactory evidence; settled persuasion."

Skipping ahead, the sixth definition is from a Samuel Pepys' diary, 1699, and later picked up by Samuel Johnson in his 1752 dictionary: "the finding or proving of a person guilty" of a crime.

This brings up the issue of seemingly opposite or unrelated meanings of the same word—here, an evolution of sorts over a 200-year period. This presents a rabbit hole I didn't want to go down now. But would it be fertile ground in another inquiry, or is it so tangential to our current discussion as to be irrelevant?

David

# 21. *Davar* and *Logos*: the Ambiguity of the Word

David,

Allow me to take up first your comments on how the word *conviction* seems to change in meaning (according to the OED) through history. I think this is central to our thinking (not just a detour), and I am pleased you have offered the insight.

As you indicate, the word *conviction* seems at first to refer to a strong belief (a positive connotation usually in this context), but later also takes on the negative connotation of guilt (a person with a conviction is a *convict*). It would be fascinating to trace the history of the word in terms of cultural changes, how we got from strong belief to criminal activity, but that is far beyond my ability. It does remind me, however, of the word *cell*. The monk's cell was used for contemplation, meditation, reading. But the prison cell, which should perhaps be used for contemplation and meditation, is usually just a place to lock up and punish the convicted. The two words do seem connected in terms of history and cultural change.

What is particularly interesting to me about these words in the context we have been developing is that we have words here that seem to embody opposites. The opposites perhaps emerge through cultural shifts, but it is possible to imagine that the antithetical meanings in each word are present from the beginning.

There is an early essay by Freud called "The Antithetical Meaning of Primal Words." In it, he offers a long list of words from several different languages that embody opposite meanings. The word *sacer*, for example, can mean "sacred" or "scapegoat." The word *massah* can mean "uplift" or "burden." And so on. His point seems to be that these words manifest one meaning but carry the opposite meaning in a "latent" state. The words reveal and conceal.

Primal words that contain opposites

Freud did not say much more about this in terms of words, but this is probably the beginning of his extensive theory of the dream world, dream interpretation, and so on. He argued, for example, that dreams are often filled with negative images that mean something positive. The negative dream takes on its opposite.

I think there is a connection here with poetry (and literary language in general). Perhaps that kind of wording is a kind of dreaming. We dream with the poem or story, which always seems to reveal and conceal, as we turn it and turn it, seeking ourselves within it. Each word is ambivalent, as we are; like us, it contains opposites. Two words together make up a story. And so do the opposites embedded in a single word, perhaps. The relation between belief and guilt (in *conviction*); the relationship between the place of the monk and the place of the criminal (in *cell*). There are not only opposites but stories and possibilities there

In one of her many sparkling essays, Cynthia Ozick asserts that Freud did not go far enough back in his development of psychoanalysis. It is a casual remark on her part, but thanks to my recent years of inconvenience, I now have some understanding of what she must have been thinking. For most of my life as a literature professor, I shared Freud's problem: the Greeks set the boundary. *Oedipus*, the Greek philosophers, the Western tradition as it developed, were central to whatever truth could be discovered as we progressed into the future. We then moved forward from the Greeks and the Romans, through the Church fathers and the Middle Ages, emerged through the progressive Enlightenment, and furthered our knowledge in the great age of science and modernism, but we forgot what we didn't desire to remember, excluded as much as we included. And even when science became scientism, yes, there was still *Oedipus* and the Oedipus Complex, and, as I often discussed in my classroom, John Keats's "Ode on a Grecian

Urn." Wasn't it the finest lyric poem ever written in English? And, yes, perhaps it still is—within our defined cultural space, at least.

Ozick might have been mistaken about Freud, though. His essay about primal words indicates a fascination with words that can be traced back through many languages. Single words that contain within them opposites: *good* and *bad, wait* and *hurry, high* and *deep*. How could anybody using reason alone possibly understand these words' meaning? Perhaps if they were accompanied by rituals or gestures? Perhaps if they were spoken in a specific context, the philosopher Ludwig Wittgenstein could have used Freud's theory as part of his own theory of "word games"?

(And, yes, perhaps Freud himself could have cited Groucho Marx's "Hello, I must be going"—if he had had an opportunity to see the Marx Brothers' movie *Animal Crackers*?)

My guess, though, is that Freud knew that these primal words were on the far side of Greek, and so he did not pursue their implications further. If he had, he would have had to enter the Hebrew tradition, the saying of the fathers: "Turn it and turn it, and turn it again, everything is there."

Is my account of Freud's thinking historically accurate? Perhaps now only in my dream place. But Freud was always concerned that his development of psychoanalysis would be rejected as a crazed Jewish theory. To protect his work, he later wrote *Moses and Monotheism*, insisting that Moses was not Jewish but Egyptian, and was in fact killed by the Jews to hide this secret. Interestingly, Freud called this work "historical fiction." Was it another attempt by Freud to distance himself and his groundbreaking work from the harsh criticism of mainstream thinking? It might have happened that way.

Allow me now, David, to return to my earlier attempt to distinguish the terms *Hebrew* and *Greek* in the kind of dream context that I have been trying to contextualize here. For me, as writers like Thorlief Boman have made clear, those words are also connected to *davar* and *logos*, and so their use becomes a necessary shorthand for a glimpse into this dream world. That glimpse might require another book, if it were only possible. That other book would include a detailed tracing of the different trajectories of these two words through the Western tradition, how *logos* buried *davar* within the West, and the way post-modernism eventually dismantled *logos* and opened a space for *davar* to reappear.

Of course, it is impossible to get back to Hebrew without going through Greek, just as it is impossible to make an original reading of the Hebrew Bible without an endless de-creative reading and rereading of the New Testament. At times, the best literary writing, I think, helps us at least to explore such differences. But I am not so much interested in the return as in the going forth: how we might read now—the silence and the voice and what is in between, that is, within the words that allow us to dream. Perhaps we can find it today in the gap (the silence) between the following two quotations, one modern (from Emmanuel Levinas) and one ancient (from the Gospels):

> It is to the extent that the word refuses to become flesh that it assumes a presence among us. (Levinas)

> The word became flesh and dwelt among us. (John)

What is the distinction, then, between Hebrew and Greek, *davar* and *logos*, Judaism and the Greco-Christian West, as I am thinking about it? If you look up the word *davar* on a recently developed artificial intelligence (AI) website, you will read that *davar* and *logos* are basically the same. They both translate as "word." The last sentence on that popular website reads: "Both words point to the person and work of Jesus Christ as the ultimate expression of God's word." For me, David, that is the problem (but not a solution).

To me, *davar* calls up the multidimensional experience of the movement of language. As I indicated before, it means "word" and "deed" and "action." All of that and more in this one word. *Davar* presses endlessly forward and suggests remembrance and ritual. It does not point to something seen as much as it serves as a promise, a type of covenant between I and thou, an inspiration for ongoing questioning and dialogue, a way to further interpretation. *Davar* interests the reader in the particularity of each thing, as some scholars have said, emphasizing the uniqueness rather than the essence of everything. It privileges the flow of concrete personal experience in the world.

I am not suggesting that, in 2024, *davar* should stand alone without *logos*, any more than speech and poetry should abandon logical reason and philosophy. But if there is a relationship between *davar* and *logos*, Hebrew and Greek, the difference should also be sorted out.

I embrace the recent and painstaking work of Iain McGilchrist in *The Matter with Things*, his two-volume, 1,500-page work concerning the right brain and the left brain. He does not address the words *davar* or *logos* directly, but he does make it very clear that the problem we now face within the Western tradition is that the left hemisphere has a stranglehold on the right hemisphere, that scientific and technical reason, now brought to its extreme, blocks the creative energy and dynamic flow of the right brain. There was a time, McGilchrist insists, when the right hemisphere was the master and the left hemisphere kept it from too much overflow, and since the earliest times all human beings have had both sides of the brain working in some kind of dialogical compatibility. For him, the master was the right brain, the emissary was the left brain. For me, this is somewhat like saying that *davar*, with its sense of rhythm and sound, of bodily and personal poetic language, of semantic flow and imaginative possibilities, has over time been hijacked by the more abstract and disembodied logic of *logos*. It is as if *davar* has slowly been buried in *logos*. The result has been that abstract conceptual thought has too often developed into frozen ideologies, abstractions, and pictorial images on screens masquerading as closed-off truths, idols worshipped as gods.

Today, in the midst of the development of AI, the power of virtual reality, and the trumping of embodied language by the rule of the disembodied image, I can only dream about the possibility of the impossible—that perhaps we will have dialogue between *davar* and *logos* that honors and respects the profound difference between the two, the saying and the said, the telling and the told. Yet perhaps it is possible?—when we move through time which moves through us. Perhaps the unhoped hope will yet arrive through the ongoing translation of ourselves and the world around us.

Scholars claim that the Greek Heraclitus first described *logos* as "order from above." But ironically it was probably Philo of

Alexandria, a renowned Jewish philosopher, who popularized the term. Philo apparently did not know Hebrew, but, like Freud, he often wrote to protect the Jews as well as to develop his work contributing to the important expansion of Greek thinking. He was, in fact, one of the few Jews granted Greek citizenship. Scholars speculate that the work of St. Paul was heavily influenced by what Philo had to offer. As Philo put it at one point in his career, drawing on his often typical style of double purpose for two different audiences, the *logos* is "the first begotten son of the uncreated Father."

For me, *davar* creates its own trajectory through translation and time. It carries with it the possibility that the saying and the making of events and things can happen simultaneously. Perhaps it is the voice in the breath of the language that I hear, a sense of what is, what is not, and what ought to be.

In other words, for me, *Davar* suggests the word as a kind of creative energy infused with the breath, more a verb in action rather than a noun at rest. Since the Tower of Babel, we might imagine, it is best enacted through generous and responsible dialogue, always open and incomplete. It hovers in the gaps of narrative time, resonates with someone moving back and forth in prayer (*davening*) or with the Yeshiva students, moving about and gesturing with their hands, as they joyously argue about a passage from the Talmudic texts.

The verb in action versus the noun at rest

As Yoram Hazony suggests in *The Philosophy of Hebrew Scripture*, how do we know what is "true friendship," how do we know it is "good," how do we know it is reliable? Only through the enactment of time.

To me now, *davar* carries a sense of absence as well as a possibility. Perhaps it roams at times like the doe of dawn at the edge of the forest just before the break of dawn. As readers paying close attention to each word in its sound and its movement, we are invited to dream next to it, to respond to its silence and its voice.

To put it another way, as the scholar McGilchrist explains it, it is only with the late discovery of the definite article *the* (a grammatical construct not found in the earlier Koine Greek) that *good* suddenly becomes *the Good*. That is, the word *good* then becomes an abstract immoveable noun undercutting what the Biblical God might have meant when He simply expressed pleasure in His creation by saying, "it is very good."

For me then, in my dream world at least, in contrast to *davar*, *logos* implies recollection more than remembrance. There are similarities no doubt, but as I have said, I am interested in differences as well. Recollection, in my view, hints at a collection fitted together like an old family album. It keeps a distance and threatens to block the flow from the past to the future, threatens a kind of stuckness or a nostalgic look backward. It invites a gathering together for philosophical contemplation, tranquility for thought. In Latin, it takes the form of two words, as many have said: *res* and *verbum*, "thing" and "word," exacerbating the split between the letter and the spirit, the literal and the figurative, provoking support for the kind of allegorical and figurative reading that even the charitable Augustine wrestled with, including the notion that the Old Testament should, with rare exception, be read primarily as a sign of news that could be discovered in the New Testament pointing to the good.

In this context, the noun outstrips the verb, the word and the object become increasingly distinct, seeing trumps listening, images and statues seem favored rather than the flow of stories, what things look like is privileged over the process of seeing how they are made. In other words, rather than enter into the rhythmic movement of the polysemous word through time, we use the word as a sign that points to the thing. In such an environment, time itself also seems to take on a different pattern; time is viewed as past / present / future—a type of spatial arrangement similar to signs on a map or dates on a calendar. It is as if time becomes abstract, not personal.

To put this in still other terms, I would suggest that *logos*, especially when translated through Athenian philosophy as "reason," attempts to privilege stability and permanent being through a belief in cause / effect relations; the world is a thing that words point to and so can be categorized in the pursuit of the Truth and the Good. But at what cost?

In my dream world, I can only conclude that over time *logos* anchors the Western tradition along the lines I have offered here. It becomes a picture of the Greek city-state and many years later, the picture of the American "city on a hill." A rather exclusive picture of democracy under the law of reason. It is a brilliant dreamscape no doubt, but one that today has been called into question, in part, because it has been severely reduced by scientism and by unmitigated power and narrowly focused bureaucratic logic. But also because the human, for better and for worse, is not an entity of reason alone. Our discussions about the Holocaust, David, leave little doubt about that.

*Davar* is different from *logos*, just as Hebrew is different from Greek. If *logos* reminds us at times that human language is a fallen language, *davar* reminds us today that it is not so much a fallen language as a language with an infinite gap that calls for dialogue and serious discussion. The world is filled with pain and suffering, but it is nevertheless a world of language and interpretation, a world with promise, call and response, infinite dialogue. It is a vulnerable and fragile world, but yet one with stories, messy and mysterious as life itself.

And this, then, is the work of the reader as much as the writer: to rejuvenate the words that circulate like dead things in the gap between the extremes of silence and of voice. The reader and the writer listen for the whisper, the trace, the spark, the fragments of *davar* within that gap that might yet provide opposition to those dead things. Bending forward to listen, the literary writer and the engaged reader with desire and eros work to rejuvenate the language. They struggle to evoke the multidimensional words of creative energy that might just change our lives, might just move us from the pull of thanatos.

The work of reader and writer: to find and respond to the fragments of *davar*

Spin the word and you will discover something different each time. Infinity in a grain of sand. The world in a word. I am reminded of *Richard III*, and his "I am determined to be a villain." What does *determined* mean here? That Richard will be the personal agent of his own villainous action? That he is determined to do that—yes. But it might very well be that this is his destiny—not his personal determination, but his given fate (he has been "determined" by destiny).

We map our dreams, our story, our life onto the poetry and stories that we read, and what we discover, if we are serious, is something (as you have said, David) that we did not know about ourselves. This is risky and dangerous, but also often both shocking and rewarding. I think of the act of reading in this context as a process of translation. It is a kind of transgression (but not, as Harold Bloom liked to say, a "misreading"). There is always something revealed, but also something concealed in the language, a mystery or a secret that hints at something more. Something left over. Something forgotten, lost or overflowing, hidden in the words.

Let me give you a different kind of example. People often tell me that the name I gave to our prison program Changing Lives Through Literature borders on a kind of blasphemy, even idolatry. How could I claim that literature changes lives? If convicts going through the program were less likely to reoffend, that was not due to the literature. Indeed, Harold Bloom once said to me that "literature is pleasurable, but it has no moral value." Of course, I am mindful of the line from Rilke's "Archaic Torso of Apollo": "You must change your life." I disagreed with Bloom; literature can carry a creative healing power.

Most, I would assume, take that Rilke meant that you must change your life *for the better*. But perhaps he meant that you should not change your life *for what people mistakenly think is better for you*. Perhaps Rilke simply meant to make your life different. After all, it is your one unique precious life. Spin the word. Everything is in it.

Spin the word—for better or for worse

Allow me now to go back (or forward?) again to our early discussion of Adorno and Steiner, and the issue of silence in regards to the Holocaust. Words can protect us, but we cannot forget the dead in that horror. Yet we cannot pretend to know what the experience of their terror and death really was like. They are "the others" whom we must acknowledge and remember. But we cannot represent their experience without a lot of guilt on our part, and their experience remains a secret which will never be revealed, except perhaps by the silence between the words, the open wound of a loss that cannot be spoken—perhaps only in the dreams which we call nightmares. It is somewhat like our own pain, the pain we experience because we are mortal, the pain that we cannot explain because we know we will die but cannot represent our own deaths. But, despite Adorno, we cannot give up trying.

Critic Elaine Scarry says we dream with the book. We need words (language) to stay alive. It remains our job, I think, to try to write something new in order to contribute our story to the ongoing life of all the stories in the universe. The gap between what we imagine we know and the secret itself provides space for our story if we are courageous enough to try to create something in that gap. To write what is not yet written—call it, as Philip Roth has, "the as-yet unwritten"—that is part of the work. We are all guilty and we are all implicated. It is perhaps the honesty of serious readers and writers to encounter the uniqueness of their story, an offer to others as well, a new possibility, an expanded horizon to consider and interpret.

Not ideology or false idols but ongoing dialogue moves us forward. The words of the literary artist give us hope in this regard. Not redemption, not ideology, but possibilities. Not optimism, but not nihilism either. Possibilities, ultimately, through a covenant, a promise through words, writer to reader and back again. That is the wonder of life and the enchantment of literature and dreams.

Bob

# 22. "Can You Describe This?"

Bob,

T he remarkable ground you covered in your last! Freud, Heraclitus, Hebrew, *Richard III*, and more.

I suppose I return anew to what language can do, has done, must do. A source has it that, in the 1660s, Robert Hooke, English polymath, looked through a primitive microscope at a thin-cut piece of cork. He saw a series of walled boxes that reminded him of the tiny rooms, or *cellula*, occupied by monks. He therefore called these tiny building blocks "cells"—and it was a short leap to calling our own body's small walled boxes by the same name.

Can you imagine the absolutely stunning meta-surprises that early practitioners of microscopes, including Hooke, encountered? More so perhaps even than those using early telescopes to look upward, though if I have it right Galileo was at the cutting edge of both. So, in the early 1600s, people's concepts of the micro, with tiny building blocks, and the macro, with planets circling the sun, were completely altered. No wonder conservative forces (the Catholic Church for one) were at wit's end.

Question for us: was language up to the task of capturing these revolutions in observation and thought? And how interesting that Shakespeare was midcareer during this intellectual upheaval. Do we know whether and how he was influenced by it?

As for prisons, early American Quakers particularly liked the concept of the soul being improved through solitary meditation.

And for a convict, ideally in a cell not unlike those used by monks, self-reflection would lead to penance—hence the term *penitentiary*, a place not for punishment, but for a process of spiritual growth and renewal. (How cruelly antiquated that idea feels now.)

A cell confines; can it also, somehow, liberate?

None other than Benjamin Franklin put all this in a pamphlet promoting the construction of a house of repentance, in which solitude could work to soothe the minds of criminals—an enlightened alternative to inhumane public punishments like the gallows, the pillory, the stocks, the whipping post, and the wheelbarrow. (Yes, convicts were chained to wheelbarrows for very long periods of time, as convicts were chained to galley oars.)

To revisit monks for a moment: I do believe that for them the cell was a place with positive meaning. In Shakespeare, Friar Laurence in his cell is not being confined against his will, but rather, I'm sure that, being a free man, he enjoyed a place to retreat to and pursue quiet contemplation. How else could he come up with his plan to unite Romeo and Juliet using herbs and a potion?

You and I both have had experience bringing something positive to prison inmates, and thus have seen close-up what punitive confinement is and does. Wasn't the schoolroom practice of sitting someone in the corner, facing where two walls come together, close to confinement in a cell? Then add the dunce cap, and you've got full-blown medieval scorn and humiliation. I understand some U.S. school systems are going back to corporal punishment with paddles (if indeed they ever ceased), reviving the primitive Christian trope that the body is a house of evil, home to the devil, and must therefore suffer. The conservative commentator William F. Buckley, on taking up physical exercise in midlife, called it "mortification of the flesh." Kill the devil by killing the body. Hello, capital punishment.

While dwelling on imprisonment, I want to add that I think what you did—bringing literature behind prison walls, exposing inmates to the healing and humanizing nature of the printed word—was exemplary. I would have liked to be the proverbial fly on the wall for those sessions, or better, a participant with you.

Connections
among people
are built
through trust—
and trust goes
deeper than
words

For myself, the Alternative to Violence Project that Sharon, myself and a group of like-minded, mostly Quaker people brought into prison was one of the most profound experiences of my life. Our three-day workshops, with twenty-five inmates in a circle slowly trusting us to explore peaceful conflict resolution with them, inevitably went broad and deep. Looking back on it, I see that language, while crucial to the process, in a way was not the primary driver of connection. Rather, it was trust, shown but not spoken, that broke down barriers. For one who loves language, and makes it a primary tool of life, it was a humbling experience.

To take a hard turn, I'm on to the subject of words with opposite meanings, and to build on your thinking on this, and your example of *Richard III* ("I am determined to be a villain."). Your thought intrigues me no end. Oh, for my OED. Absent it, I'll wing it a little, paraphrasing the conventional definition of *determined* as something like "having made a firm decision and being resolved not to change it." Yet the philosophy we call Determinism posits that all events, including human action, are ultimately decided by causes external to the will.

Can it be that Shakespeare's Richard adheres to this philosophy? Is he saying that his actions are not the result of his own will at all? If this were true, the whole premise of Western justice is bogus, no? What if a murderer—or his lawyer—were to claim his actions were not the result of his will, but were predetermined for him? I think that's when the murderer is removed as mentally impaired, and his lawyer finds another line of work.

And what of the very Shakespearean concept of trial by combat? We see it over and over—in *Richard III, Macbeth, Henry VI, Henry IV,* and elsewhere—in which the process of deciding who dies and who lives to become king is a sword fight. Is the winner simply demonstrating against that might makes right, or is the premise that fate, God, or some other controlling deity will intervene to make sure the correct (good) combatant wins, i.e., that Determinism is indeed the abiding force ensuring a morally correct outcome? Morally correct in whose eyes? God's. And therefore highly acceptable to the royal family that continues to reign.

I certainly see how the Enlightenment, and its bedfellow, rationalism, turned that around. If it hadn't, and I decided it was fated that I not pay my bills (or honor my word) and therefore am free to do otherwise . . . well, Donald Trump, have at it.

Your ruminations on language and the silence around Holocaust victims haunt me. To quote you:

> Yet we cannot pretend to know what the experience of their terror and death really was like. They are "the others" whom we must acknowledge and remember. But we cannot represent their experience without a lot of guilt on our part.

How do we square this with the sanctity and power of the word? When I was struggling to capture a dire moment in my novel *Under Pegasus* and wondering if all experience can indeed be captured truthfully in telling, my neighbor and friend, novelist Hugh Nissenson, told me, "Anything a human has experienced can be told, as long as the telling is honest." That was his faith, and I guess mine too. Without that faith, would Dante ever have rendered, in words, his pilgrim's experience through hell to paradise? Or Eliot have taken us into his spiritually bereft world? Or Kafka into his bleak nightmare-scape?

If our world were seared beyond recognition tomorrow in nuclear war, would we have faith that someone, somewhere, would, or could, memorialize it in language?

In that spirit, I revert to something you wrote earlier, that could well be a defining epigraph for our book: The words of a literary artist give us hope. Here is the full quote:

> It is perhaps the honesty of serious readers and writers to encounter the uniqueness of their story, an offer to others as well, a new possibility, an expanded horizon to consider and interpret.
>
> Not ideology or false idols but ongoing dialogue moves us forward. The words of the literary artist give us hope in this regard. Not redemption, not ideology, but possibilities.

Now, on dreams: As you've also said:

There is always something revealed, but also something concealed in the language, a mystery or a secret that hints at something more. Something left over. Something forgotten, lost or overflowing, hidden in the words.

So well observed! In response, may I step back and ask, *what are dreams?* Freud thought they were suppressed wishes. Considering this, one normally jumps to a scenario where an average, or essentially good person dreams wishes that he or she considers not good, unwholesome, bad.

But what of evil, violent, destructive people. Wouldn't it be fascinating to know the dreams of Jack the Ripper, Joseph Stalin, Adolf Hitler? Could their dreams be impulses they have repressed, that were likeable, serene, and altruistic impulses?

Similarly, dreams of famously very good people—St. Francis, Albert Schweitzer, Mother Teresa—what of them? Were those dreams violent, nasty, immoral?

Seeking meaning in the stories our dreams tell us

As to our own dreams: mine tend to be narratives involving a search for a thing lost, a person in need of finding a key to a life puzzle, a wished-for epiphany in hiding. Shall I chalk this up to my fascination with such themes in life and literature? Additionally, my dreams are narrative rather than impressionistic: a reflection of my love of novels and epics, and my preference for poetry with some kind of narrative drive? (Whitman over Emily Dickinson, Shakespeare over John Donne, Anthony Hecht over W.S. Merwin.)

Not that I don't look for the repressed wish. It might be there and I can't see it. Which brings up another interesting issue: what, as writers, as people, we can and cannot see. Clearly, we want insights that matter, that represent the best in us, in the sense of most authentic and most original. Yet what if our best thoughts lie just beyond us, like a nighttime road's tree-lined course just beyond our headlights' range?

And what of language and dreams? If I try to record a dream by writing it down, I'm inevitably left with what feels like a crude outline or precis and not by any means the whole dream, and I'm bereft of subtleties and nuances that I instinctively know made the dream meaningful. How to live with that? Humility and an acknowledgement of one's limitations may be the essential starting point.

Branching off from Freud (or doing an abrupt 90-degree turn): Carl Jung, on the way to arriving at his ideas of the collective unconscious, shared realities populated by instincts as well as by archetypes. He of course thought deeply about dreams, not just in *Memories, Dreams, Reflections*, but also in *The Red Book*, his stunning compendium of drawings and paintings. One of his ideas: "The dream shows the inner truth and reality of the patient as it really is: not as I conjecture it to be, and not as he would like it to be, but as it is."

This seems quite the challenge to both thought and language. What writer has the fortitude to write about herself in terms of what actually is (regarding, say, decisions and values) vs. what she would like it to be? (Yes, Jung uses "patient," begging the question of his thought being relevant to a non-patient. Or are we, in his view, all patients?)

On to Rilke and "you must change your life." I appreciate your analysis of the word "change" in this context—change for better, change for worse? I have always, perhaps simplistically, experienced this line as a non sequitur at the end of the poem. I understand the two "Otherwise" lines . . . meaning if the torso was not lighted from within, certain realities would not follow. But why, as the reader, must I change my life in reaction to this?

Lastly, to silence.

Anna Akhmatova, in her 1957 *Requiem*, recounts that, during the Yezhof terror (also called the Great Purge), she spent considerable time outside a prison in Leningrad, as an act of bearing witness. One day, a woman approached her and whispered, "Can you describe this?" Akhmatova replied, "Yes I can," then observed that "something like the shadow of a smile crossed the woman's face."

*Can you describe this?* Perhaps the eternal question. And a poet says she can, then does. What drove her? I'd posit, that the alternative—silence—was the true enemy, along with Stalin, and therefore unacceptable. Silence can't win, or we've traded in our humanity.

Bearing witness: the eternal challenge

After all, all we need are our eyes, hands, and a small mix of energy and courage . . . or maybe not even courage, but anger and desperation.

May we never be tested as Akhmatova was, but if we are, well—I pray that we'll know what to do. And maybe someone will show the shadow of a smile.

David

# 23. Covenant of Writer and Reader

David,

Where to begin now after some further lapse of time? Why not back to the beginning, after this gap in our conversation? Forward to the beginning of your poem by the pool:

> The music returns
> And so I return to music by the pool . . .

From where does the music originate? I want to return to that question now with a renewed hunch. Perhaps it originates from "no place," before space or time: call it immemorial time, if you like.

Perhaps from that nothingness before the beginning, the *aleph* before the *bet* in the Hebrew alphabet, before creation, before the trauma of birth (the trauma of the world, the trauma of our unique life, the trauma of history)?

Giorgio Agamben has suggested (in *Language and Death*), that when the early Greek rhetoricians used the word *topos* (topics), they originally meant "no place," the place of nothingness. Later the troubadours focused on *amour* (love and desire) in an attempt to find this no place.

At times, I think about this no place as the place of the immemorial past, the place that cannot be recovered or grasped, but which the poets in particular search for through history. It is the place that is and is not, the no place at the edge of creation.

The Greek Muses helped the poets, inspired them to move close to this edge of creation. It is as if the poet, guided by the Muse, comes to a kind of boundary or bar that he leans across, listening intently for this nothingness, this silence which arouses him to respond with music and song. It is as if he patiently waits for the call and then goes forth in response with word and deed.

Such poets sing with breath and voice, with desire and yearning, creating a sublime dizziness that surpasses what the Greek Parmenides thought of as reason, what philosophy thinks of as propositions. The poets go forth to the edge of the liminal, the sublime imagination, attempting to bring a new birth into the ongoing plot of history.

Perhaps some of what I am saying here is connected to the music you heard sitting poolside not long ago—the music that became a poem that helped renew a conversation first begun in Mead House at Brown in 1962.

But the Greek Muse, and memory itself, are only part of the story I am now thinking about. I wonder, for example, whether there is a difference between the *topos* and the Muse of the Greeks (on the one hand) and the desert of the Israelites, a no place of infinite endlessness. I have recently been reading a book by Ranen Omer-Sherman called *Israel in Exile: Jewish Writing And the Desert*, which I have found very helpful in this regard. As he suggests, the desert is a place open to the roar of the voice, the thunder and lightning above the mountain top, the sands forever shifting and twirling in the wind (as the poet Jabès puts it). Does the desert evoke a different kind of imagination than the imagination of the Greeks? A different response and different inspiration?

Writers like Omer-Sherman and poets like Jabès certainly think so. I think so, too. Call it a difference in degree, if not in kind, but there is a difference. In this regard, it is also interesting to consider that the Hebrew word *midbar* (which can mean "wilderness" or "desert," and can imply wandering and exile) finds its root in the word *davar*. Not a mere coincidence, I am sure.

Permit me an exaggeration, reasonable perhaps but overextended to make my point. The difference I am thinking about is

the difference between Hebrew and Greek, as someone like Boman and many others (Eric Auerbach, Emmanuel Levinas,
Jacques Derrida, for example) have suggested. It is the difference
between "going forth" (like the biblical Abraham) and "returning
home" (like the epic hero Odysseus).

As I've said countless times now, *davar* means "word" but also
"deed" and "thing." For me, it is a word that suggests a promise
rather than what is seen, movement more than contemplation,
dialogue rather than ideal sight, the present as possibility and responsibility for work not complete rather than the totality of
some universal idea. It is open to infinite possibilities, endless
interpretation, a going forth, even a wandering and rambling
about. *Logos*, by contrast, suggests the return home, an in-gath-
ering rather than a scattering, the totality and the end.

In this context, Davar reminds me of the diaspora, exile,
wandering, incompletion, open to the movement onwards, a
sense of difference, respect for the eachness of each. *Logos* is
closer to "the same," to reason, the essence, the established order
and supposed substance of being.

As I have been suggesting, *logos* is Greek, tends towards philosophy and Athens, and has had a profound influence on Christian and Western thought and culture. Its emphasis is on the image, sculpture, the visible, the spirit made flesh. *Davar* favors the
not seen, listening rather than seeing, call / response rather than
logic and propositions. *Davar* indicates movement and so a kind
of blur; *logos* prefers contemplation and stillness, a clear picture.

I connect the long history of discussion and thought about
the relation and distinction between Jerusalem and Athens with
this kind of thinking. Such discussion stretches back at least as
far as the famous question asked by Tertullian, the Latin church
father: "What does Athens have to do with Jerusalem?" Much
later, the Russian thinker Lev Shestov (*Athens and Jerusalem*)
agreed with Tertullian, arguing (with some irony) that Athens
kept us enslaved to "the chains of Parmenides" (the belief in the
necessity of reason and the logic of being), while the faith in Jerusalem, as absurd as it was, according to Shestov, could open us
to freedom and life itself. We could give up the illusion of the
tree of good and bad and go forth towards the tree of life.

Going forth
versus
returning
home: two
wellsprings of
literary
creation

Mathew Arnold (*Culture and Anarchy*) also distinguished between Hebrew and Hellene from a different angle, but he too emphasized the difference. For him, contrasting the two was a way to talk about the moral law in tension with aesthetic beauty. And then in a brilliant essay years later, Erich Auerbach (*Mimesis*) in a chapter called "Odysseus' Scar," offered significant insight into the difference between the mimetic style of the story of Abraham and Isaac with its gaps and background, its silences and invisibility, and the story of Odysseus, with its strong and typical Greek foregrounding and clear visibility.

By the time that the so-called deconstructionists, like Jacques Derrida, appear on the scene, the *logos*, both in its Greek and Christian context, has undergone radical challenges. For Derrida, both Greek philosophy and Christian theology (the law of contradiction and the word become flesh) have literalized the fundamental value of transition and translation. Both Greek philosophy and Christian dogma have become idol worship in a Western world privileging the visual rather than the voice, incarnation over the no place. For Derrida and others, the thing smothers the voice, eventually destroys language, controls the word. Words become commodities.

But where do we seek the no place, I now ask. Here's a list of possibilities that I sometimes dream about:

Where can
we find the
no place?

1. In the unseen Garden of Eden
2. In the endless shifting and whispering of desert sands (Jabès)
3. Above the mountain top (Sinai or Snowden)
4. In the unseen voice (with its thousands of voices)
5. In the wind (Shelley and Dylan)
6. In unknown burial plots (from Moses to the Holocaust)

From the no place emerges the white light of day, the voiceless voice that provides background for history and language. For the Hebrew, the decisive reality of the world of experience (as Boman says) then becomes "the effective word," human language constant and infinite in its movement and flow, dynamic and almost a blur, always going forth in dialogue towards the other. By contrast, for the Greeks, the word becomes a gathering

100

together, a reckoning, a homecoming; for Christians, perhaps, it becomes substance and arrangement, clear and visible.

It is possible to say that the post-modern world is a world of exile, of wandering, and of going forth without the acknowledgment of return. The homeless and the refugees are perhaps the best measure of what the no place has really become. I am reminded, though, not so much of the Greeks right now or the homeless, but of the biblical text "He sits and roars." Perhaps it has always been like this. Perhaps a more reasonable example is that wonderful passage in George Eliot's *Middlemarch*:

> If we had a keen vision in human life, it would be like hearing the grass grow, or the squirrel's heart beat and we should die of that roar which is the other side of silence.

To me, this all suggests that language, at least as we know it, especially the language of literature, not philosophy or propositions, not the language of judgment or reason, but the language of poetry and narrative, is a going-forth more than a return home. It reaches out to the other, the place that we do not know (within and without, the no place, the in-between). It calls to the stranger, it is a response to a friend, to the invisible as much as, if not more than, the visible.

Literary language goes forth (like Abram turned Abraham) toward the no place, the boundless, the limitless, the voice on the other side of silence (as George Eliot puts it). But literary language also protects us from that roar. Without that protection, the world would collapse (and we with it). History would end.

Wittgenstein put it this way: "The limit of our language is the limits of our world." Wittgenstein did not say that there is no place beyond language, but implied that language is a blessing, a gift that can help us defend our humanity, a covenant between the invisible and the visible. It gives us borders, limits, so we are not swallowed up in the boundless roar of what is beyond our grasp and comprehension.

This is not to argue that we are locked in some kind of prison house of language. It is possible that literary language in particular is not even wrapped in time, but rather produces time. This is part of its supreme value—let's say, its metaphoric value.

For me, valuable literary work includes the work of metaphor (as I understand it). It struggles against the illusion of the literal, the constant danger of the creative word collapsing into a commodity to be bought and sold. Our personal utterance, when honest and unique, makes something new in the world, just as each person born into this world represents something new, a new word to help articulate and expand the unfolding story of the world.

And we read as we write. Each reading is a new reading; each rereading is a new reading as well. To me, it is much like Abraham after the destruction of the Tower of Babel. Abraham crossing over the Jordan, an act of translation, a crossing-over and a going-forth. Despite what many think, what we call metaphor emphasizes difference rather than sameness. It resonates with a sense of difference, a uniqueness, a singularity, which might not be better than what came before but offers a new perspective, a new possibility for attention and further questioning. I consider metaphor as a relationship in motion, between the personal utterance and the voices of others, between the personal and the social, the visible and the invisible, all in an ongoing dialogue that is best considered a promise and a blessing.

Metaphor as a tool for breaking boundaries

Metaphor is crucial in this context. It is a going-forth and a crossing-over, a questioning of the established boundaries, a transgression in the quest for something different, something new and unique. Metaphor works to keep language alive, struggles against the copy and the cliché, works to suggest a new possibility. Metaphor shakes up what we thought was necessary, breaks the ice and stones, bricks and cement of the frozen heart. It is Abraham's crossing of the Jordan River summoning the reader in the present tense.

Parmenides insisted that to think there was anything but the "is" of "being" was unreasonable. But metaphor emphasizes the particular more than the same, not essence but connectivity, the tension between the eachness and the not-yet. It opens up new choices and possibilities. It insists that being both is and is not. If it is reasonable, it is also transgressive. It protects us and sets us free, inspiring us to go forth and continue to ask questions. It is closer to a verb than a noun.

Such thinking now brings me to a brief consideration of Keats and that immortal bird celebrated in a gift I once received from you, David, a beautiful small book by Duncan Wu. In his introduction, Wu reminds the reader of the Greek myth of Philomena (whose name means "love song"). She is raped by her brother-in-law and then turned into a nightingale. The myth weaves its way through Milton's "Il Penseroso" and is transformed through the Romantic poets. The "Ode to a Nightingale" by Keats is undoubtedly the greatest poem in this tradition. It is metaphor, transgression leading toward singularity, translation with its highest implications.

My immediate interest here is that before the poem begins, we can assume, the poet has already listened to the song of the nightingale. It is, in this sense, before the beginning; it is in the no place before we, as readers, listen (with Keats) to the music of the poem (and of the nightingale itself).

When the poem opens, it is as if we experience the emerging of the event of language itself, the birth of song as Keats responds to the no place that has been calling to him. There is very little visibility here, although the poem itself is filled with ambiguity, contradictions, sensuousness, loving desire, and melancholy.

Is it possible to contrast the poem with the "Ode on a Grecian Urn" in terms I have been discussing: Hebrew vs. Greek? I think it is. The myth here is Greek: there are references in the poem to the Greeks (Bacchus, for example), but it is, to me, the surprise in the penultimate stanza that deserves special attention now:

> Perhaps the self-same song that found a path
> Through the sad heart of Ruth, when sick for home,
> She stood with tears amid the alien corn . . .

I want to suggest that the nightingale ode is a poem in sharp contrast to the Grecian urn ode. Why in the world does Keats choose the story of Ruth from the Hebrew Bible at this moment in the poem? I cannot find any nightingale in the biblical story. There is melancholy, but Keats is already thinking about his next poem (probably the "Ode to Melancholy"). Again at the risk of overgeneralization, I would suggest that this poem is Keats's Hebrew poem, mixed as it is. It is a poem of metaphor and movement, invisibility and ambiguity. It is filled with unresolved contradictions that heighten its sense of life and questioning. Most important, perhaps, it does not offer a totality nor a clear image. Rather it ends, as all great literature does, unresolved—that is, with a question: "Do I wake or sleep?"—a question accompanied by the disappearance of the nightingale itself.

Great literature ends with a question

By contrast, the "Ode on a Grecian Urn" is highly visual. The urn is an artifact that was fashionable at the time. If it is an indirect reference to the Elgin Marbles, which Keats had recently viewed with some wonder in the British Museum, the urn, nevertheless, unlike the nightingale, is a visual object of stillness, not energetic movement, and we might imagine that what Keats said about the Elgin Marbles can be applied, at its best, to the Grecian urn: "I never cease to wonder at all that incarnate Delight." It is not so much the visible urn, though, but the wonder of Keats' imagination that creates the urn for us, the wonder of language which offers room for freedom and movement for us the readers. We might say the marble urn is complete and total, closed off, but the ode is also infinite and incomplete; it continues on, even beyond the tag line "Beauty is truth, truth beauty"—a line of verse satisfying to the urn but not to the mortal human reader.

Allow me now a pause here, a fictional midrash, that I hope will help connect Keats and the other Romantics with my recent focus on Hebrew and Greek. I will return to Keats in a few minutes. Call this a brief commentary.

As I was walking through Central Park one day, I overheard two rabbis speaking.

Rabbi Arvenu said, "According to Rabbi Mendel, after Noah and the flood, God was prepared to choose a new man, a righteous one, who would be a wanderer (a Hebrew), one that had faith and that He had faith in, a man that He could make a covenant with, someone He would not have to destroy by water or fire with that incredible roar of His."

Rabbi Shim'on then said, "Yes, He could not trust a drunkard like Noah, and He knew the whole story about Shem and Japheth walking backward into Noah's bedroom was too ridiculous to believe. He needed someone He could trust, someone He could count on.

"So, as it is said, it was ten generations between Noah and Abram. That is a long time to wait for a righteous man, but I've been told that a good man is hard to find. If you don't believe me, you can see the whole list of generations marked out in the Bible. God had been waiting for ten generations to discover a righteous man. He finally found one in a fellow called Abram and then added two letters to his name. Abram became Abraham. It was almost as if the word and the man were one. Some even say it was the moment when the world moved from myth to history, from a single language to thousands of human voices . . . each with its particular distinction."

"The best thing that happened during this period was that God blew down that stupid tower that Nimrod tried to build," Rabbi Arvenu said. "Yes, He did that to punish those filled with too much hubris (a word that always makes me think about Aristotle and tragedy). Listening to a gas-lighter like Nimrod, these construction workers were convinced they could possess the heavens as well as the earth."

"Well, that is what Rabbi Mendel once said," Rabbi Shim'on asserted. "And you seem to agree. But permit me to suggest something different. God thought Nimrod, the leader for building the Tower of Babel, was like Baalam and his ass. They were all ventriloquists who did not speak the truth, just the same clichés and abstractions. Very much like the snake in the garden, the one who always pops up East of Eden now and enjoys making trouble. It reminds me of the committee meeting I attended the other day at the local synagogue. It was all abstraction, no individual voices. You know what I am talking about—an abstract judgment pushed by committee, showing no sense of freedom or responsibility. It was a hollowed-out voice, a voice of abstraction."

"So, what happened? Tell us. We're listening."

"Well, God sent the committee and the chairman packing, destroyed the tower, created separate languages, left the tower broken and scattered. It was an event of significant disruption—opening time for the freedom of individuals and choice."

The act of disruption and the gift of human freedom

Rabbi Arvenu now saw it differently. "Yes, I might not fully agree, but I cannot disagree. It is very much like what happened when Moses broke the tablets of the original Ten

Commandments. The poet William Blake, you might know, was pleased by that defiance and display of human freedom. He saw it as a worthy act of freedom and rebellion. Perhaps God did it for that reason. We can't know for sure. But we can imagine it was an opening, a way of starting history, and connecting individual language with human creation. It allowed for different perspectives and for individual questing (and questioning).

"Perhaps it allowed for the creation of writing, as well—the inscription on the second set of tablets, inspired from the first broken tablets. Both sets were carried through the desert in the Ark of the Covenant for forty years. That is a wonder."

So, at the end of ten generations, from Noah to Abram, a righteous man appears. Rabbi Shim'on explains: "He crosses over, or let's say turns away from a place of idols and shadows. God makes him the chosen one, not because he is privileged or special but because he has work to do, an assigned and chosen responsibility, a promise to keep."

Abram apparently speaks Aramaic and was an idol worshipper. But now God calls to him and even teaches him Hebrew. As Abram become Abraham, he circumcises himself and others. Creating from the freedom given him and limitations imposed on him by the covenant, Abraham becomes the uniqueness of the mortal man. Like all human beings, he is chosen now to wander and wonder, to become Abraham and nobody else.

Abraham leaves the shadows of home and the idols of his father and goes out across the river as a wanderer into the world. He begins the work of the Hebrew (the wanderer), the work of all mortals in time, the righteous as a man of words and deeds, the questioner, the faithful who can be counted on to help the others who also struggle on the quest for that which cannot be grasped. Not what is, but what is not—what can be if we wander and wonder onwards.

This is Abram translated into Abraham.

But what about Keats's "Ode to a Nightingale"? Yes, David, I have not forgotten. Although I favor Blake overall, this poem stands for me as the greatest written in English. We might say it begins before the beginning, a no place that creates the desire for an event of language ("My heart aches . . . "). Although highly sensuous, typical of Keats, the language is not so much seen as imagined, and listening to the nightingale's song provides the central rhythm and resonance for the poem and the reader. If we say that the nightingale has any substance, it is not substance that we can see but rather song as enchantment, until it passes ("The plaintive anthem fades"). It is the song that fades and is finally buried deep in the next valley-glades. This is not so much a return as it is a going forth to another no place. What Keats has captured in the poem, as he might put it, is "the pulsation of an artery."

In this context, I also note that the poem does not so much return Keats to the earth, as is usually assumed, but opens itself to a series of questions, which suggest an ongoing quest and is perhaps, at the deepest level, what a human being is determined to become. "Was it a vision, or a waking dream? Do I wake or sleep?" For Keats, the wonder comes from becoming both the questioner and the question—the human being seeking another encounter with the world and all the creatures within it.

Keats is not as clear as many readers claim he is. Shelley, by contrast, could be said to be clearer than some readers claim. For Shelley, as he puts it, "the deep truth is imageless," which is a difficult stance for a poet. Shelley, though, is also concerned with the no place. He might well be responding to Keats when he writes "To a Skylark," but his opening is reversed. He summons the skylark:

> Hail to thee, blithe spirit
> Bird thou never wert

The image of bird (an illusion) gives way to the movement of reading of the line—that is, the image is erased, the bird is no place. But Shelley carries on:

> The One remains, the many changes pass,
> Heaven's light forever shines,
> Earth's shadows fly . . .

For Shelley, "the white radiance of Eternity" seems like white light, the no light and no place that serves as background for all that we do see, all the colors that we can see due to that white light. Life, like a dome of many-colored glass, stains the white radiance of eternity, but like the darkness itself, those colors can only be seen and appreciated against the background of white light. Like Keats, though, Shelley here does not see the skylark or the white light; he listens and imagines. He enchants and is enchanted.

So, let me now ask you, David, a related series of questions:

When we speak of revelation or wonder in relation to human language or mortal life, are we talking about something heard or something seen? And are we talking about something better or simply something else, something different?

For example, what can we say about the revelation at the burning bush? The fire does not consume the bush. Moses sees the fire but turns away. The sight is too overwhelming, too frightening. But Moses also hears the voice of God and, although hesitant, responds to the divine call. We might say that revelation cannot be grasped, nor can it be fully understood. But can it be seen through the eye, or is it primarily heard through the ear? Perhaps both?

Or what about Moses receiving the Ten Commandments on Mt. Sinai: Does God hover above the mountain, dictating the words, or even inscribing them from that distance? Even if God is at the mountain top, we know that Moses does not see Him. Moses is protected by fire, thunder and lightning, clouds. At best, Moses will glimpse only the back of God, as God walks away. Perhaps only a glimpse of the trace of God, or sensing the wake of God as He disappears?

And what about the famous scene in *Anna Karenina* when Levin seems to emerge out of himself in the midst of the hayfields? It is not so much a return but rather a going forth that will make a difference forever in his life? Or "spots of time," as Wordsworth aptly called them. Not so much spatial in its image, but a "spot" that seems to melt into a timelessness. In "Tintern Abbey," for example, Wordsworth moves to "the still sad music of humanity" and so feels a presence:

> . . . a sense sublime of
> Something far more deeply interfused
> Whose dwelling is the light of setting suns . . .

A motion and a spirit, that impels
All thinking things, all objects of all thought
And rolls through all things.

Or even Joyce with his sense of epiphany?

Are these not all examples of possibilities in the present moment of language, filled with ongoing hope and desire? Not so much a return as a promise, provided we as readers have faith, that is, provided we can count on what we are reading, what we have been promised by an "other"—a trustworthy writer?

*To write is to make a promise—but can the writer be believed?*

There are, of course, moments of revelation by sight: Ezekiel seeing the chariot, for example, or the dangerous sublime beauty of the snow in Frost's "Stopping by Woods on a Snowy Evening." But it is the call and response, the listening and then the responsibility to respond to that call, that creates the foundation (if there is one) for ongoing language and mortal life.

When I wrote *The Risk of Reading*, I thought the biggest risk a reader could take was to expand consciousness outward toward the horizon. In that way, the reader might learn something more about himself, even things he might not want to know, things he ordinarily resisted. I suggested that language and words rather than images and screens could help us in this regard. I still believe that. Like no-fly zones, there should be no wi-fi zones—countercultural spaces where language and literature help us to maintain a good life and to preserve our humanity.

But I now believe that notion of risk was too narrow in its focus. The risk of reading includes both writer and reader, call and response, ongoing dialogue. A turning towards rather than a turning away. But when the writer risks pushing beyond the limit experience, the mortal boundary line itself, does he risk everything we usually call "the human"? Does he get too close? Like Aaron's sons in the temple, won't the mortal writer be struck down? Yet does the writer also risk estrangement if he takes a position at too much of a distance, like the characters in Dante's *Inferno* who are in total darkness and completely frozen? I ask you, David, my good friend—I ask you not as the inquisitor but as someone who is curious, someone who is inquisitive.

In *The Risk of Reading*, I underestimated the risk for the writer as well as the reader. Perhaps the vocation and evocation of the

Reading is
risky for both
the writer and
the reader

writer is to search for the in-between, that no place which has not yet been written, and then the event of language charged with desire emerges with the will searching for the place of human life, the in-between place, which many others have explored in their own unique way, the unwritten place between the erotic and the holy, between man and the divine, between the writer and the reader as well. The writer makes a courageous attempt to find that spot which could be considered a limit experience, not inexpressible but including an overflow of language, an overflow linked to a lack, what is missing, what is not yet graspable, what still demands the work of the creative power of human language.

The writer offers this to the reader much as a sacrifice is offered to the other. We might even say that the writing is a sacrifice, at times a dangerous one for the writer himself. But the writer is also at risk if he thinks of his writing as an exchange with payment due. He might be rejected; he might suffer anxiety because he expects a return. In such cases, we might say that he is writing for instrumental purposes, not for an end in itself. It is understandable, but at the most serious level he must risk everything. He is writing for The Other or the other, or both.

This is part of the covenant of writer and reader. But then what is the risk for the reader? Sartre said that the reader can close any book he opens. I disagree. The reader has that freedom, but he is not then a responsible reader. Once the reader encounters the book, opens it, and begins to read it, then he, too, is responsible for it. If he closes the book, puts it back on the shelf, the book collapses, loses its life, is in danger of dying. The writer might have created a character who will die in this book; the writer might have sacrificed himself for that purpose. As Walter Benjamin once said, when we close the book at the end, after the death of the main character, we realize we have not yet died; the cold corpse of the story gives us the warmth of life, the flame of living. We owe that to the writer. In this context, it is an ethical act to keep reading.

Great writing, like deep reading, transcends the capitalist market, the sense of a means to an end, the sense of the word as a commodity, the sense of popular genres. The relationship between the reader and the writer cannot be defined by market exchange. It is not the kind of risk in which we invest to get back more than we have invested, in which we win by getting on return more of the same. Both writing and reading demand self-sacrifice so we can search for our uniqueness, our difference, our destiny, which is "something else." Reading and writing might not reveal something better, but if it is honest and faithful, it will reveal something different. A risk worth taking.

In Raymond Carver's short story "Cathedral," the narrator, a man of considerable narrowness, finds himself uncomfortable with Robert, a blind man, who has been invited to his house by his wife. Late in the evening, growing somewhat comfortable with Robert, the narrator attempts to explain to him a cathedral he is seeing on television. He can't explain the sight, though, so he eventually gets a brown paper bag, and holding the blind man's hand, he guides him through the process of drawing the cathedral on the paper.

> So we kept on with it. His fingers rode my fingers as my hand went over the paper. It was like nothing in my life up to now.

The narrator continues:

> My eyes were still closed. I was in my house. I knew that. But I didn't feel like I was inside anything. "It's really something," I said.

The narrator has not returned to anything he knew before. But along with the careful, slow, and attentive reader, the narrator is beginning to explore his uniqueness, and, if the covenant holds between the writer and the reader, the reader can go forth to explore his uniqueness as well.

With close reading, the Carver story brings us to the edge of learning something new. Something else (as Carver's narrator puts it). Something different. So we can (almost) see ourselves from the outside and inside. What we are and what we are not, but also what we can be. I think that's what Philip Sidney meant long ago when he defended literature against history and philosophy. History was too specific, only offering examples of what happened. Philosophy was too abstract, too speculative. For Sidney, literature could teach and delight, and it could also move the reader to new ethical heights. We might agree that Carver also does something like that.

Perfect knowledge—to be experienced, yet never to be grasped

It might be possible that we can achieve "perfect knowledge," or at least experience such moments, although not grasp them. In *The Art of Biblical Narrative,* Robert Alter says, there is a horizon of perfect knowledge in biblical narrative but it is a horizon which we are permitted to glimpse only in the most momentary and fragmentary way. Perhaps Alter is too optimistic here, although I'd like to apply this idea to great literature in general, the kind of literature that offers complexity and contradictions, metaphors and depth, irony and vision, indirection and ambivalence. To me, the Bible too invites a similar kind of reading.

Of course, the optimism of reaching "the horizon" is in itself under ongoing attack these days, both in terms of climate change and metaphysical repositioning. Tom Stoppard recently joked: "I hope good things happen as well as bad things. You know, I'm told there is such a thing as the long view. But it never seems quite long enough to cope with the horizon."

And Tennyson, a long time ago, insisted that each time he took a step towards the horizon, the horizon seemed to take a step back: A little like moving the goal posts, which seems very much part of the modern condition. Perhaps acquiring "perfect knowledge" is an impossibility. But, nevertheless, with all my imperfections, I still want to know what I cannot know.

Bob

# 24. The Holy Wash of Language

Bob,

I enjoyed very much your analysis of Greek "returning home" vs. Hebrew "going forth," with the myriad implications both carry, and your modern examples of both (particularly Keats' "Ode to a Nightingale" over against his "Ode on a Grecian Urn"). I find your discussion of the courage of both writer and reader near the end of your comments particularly compelling.

And I must add, good friend, how what we are doing now resonates so strongly with those late-night sessions we had at Brown, with cigarettes and beer, stretching our minds to Keats, Blake, Coleridge, and beyond, discovering in them strains we no doubt felt in ourselves—indeed, were discovering in ourselves in real time—the lineaments of thought strung, as it were, on the latticework of poetry. Thus was our friendship born, and thus it continued even when set aside for long decades.

But we have it back now!

In that spirit, allow me now to respond particularly to your distinction between Hebrew and Greek.

I am drawn to your rumination on "no place," and particularly the desert of the Israelites (for them no doubt a harsh reality, for us perhaps an image, a metaphor). And you ask, does the desert evoke a different kind of imagination from that of the Greeks? For the latter, of course there is the sea (perhaps their place of nothingness) but also Greece itself; Athens as well as locales outside the city such as Colonus and Delphi, which figure so powerfully in Greek drama.

Focusing on Delphi, there is no wisdom and certainly no riddle-solving without the priestess. Can we say that without her there is a kind of nothingness in Delphi? Or is that going too far?

Hebrew going forth vs. Greek returning home: neither could exist without the respective "nothing" places—desert or sea, locales providing the expanse wherein human longing, travel, loss, and reconciliation can be acted out.

Homer's *Iliad* is a powerful going-forth, necessary for the coming-home sequel of *The Odyssey*. And, to broadly flesh this out with a close look at Greek plays for more grounding in the dynamics of travel away or returning: Iphigenia going away (*Iphigenia at Aulis*), Agamemnon coming home (*Agamemnon*), Jason returning home (*Medea*), and Medea leaving at the end for Athens, as well as Oedipus, blind or otherwise, traveling across Greece (the *Oedipus* trilogy). These and so many others forever loading up the weight of their actions, with travel as key, pushing their stories to the status of archetypes.

The meaning of *diaspora*

Of course, an individual's exile and wandering are part and parcel of it all, bringing us to the concept of diaspora, a whole population scattering. I recall no equivalent in the Greek literature, though jumping forward to the Romans, to the *Aeneid*, can we posit the action of that epic as a sort of Trojan diaspora culminating in a coming home—the founding of Rome? Or does this trivialize the Jewish diaspora? Clearly the latter stands supreme over all others for its size, its historical impact, and the definitive place it holds for an entire people.

In considering the diaspora, may I ask for a look at antisemitism in relation to it? What is its root? I inquire not as writer, nor as a scholar (which I emphatically am not) but as a gentile. One with at least a foot in Christianity (which I am by birth, but not by choice or even much by inclination). As such, do I bear responsibility for antisemitism? We know that the Romans killed Jesus, and the Jews did not. That, indeed, Christianity was initially a Jewish sect, one that but for Constantine's conversion might have remained small or even died out. (Had that happened, what would I have been at birth, and what would any of us be now?)

Which came first, the diaspora or antisemitism? No doubt, much research has been done on this.

I'm now inspired (compelled?) to explore further the music I heard by the pool as we began our conversation over a year ago. I had never before been to that pool, but I see now that it became for me all pools or bodies of water that I had known.

So, in late 2022, we had this:

> And so I return to music by the pool
> and watch the water's blue ripples
> kiss and kiss again the pool's concrete walkway.
>
> The sun passes overhead, eyes the pool,
> extends down transparent fingers to touch
> the ripples (a solar kiss or act of ownership?)
> till nightfall will send it packing.

Now I feel an urgency to finish the poem:

> And so I sit, eyes not venturing to search for the sun—
> never daring to look right at it (protecting
> me from a final act of perfect, blinding sight).
> Instead, I search sky, grass, pool's concrete
> walkway and the reflected light atop the water's
> ripples. While ears, passive, wait and wait
> again for music—the beat and hum of strings
> and drum. While, finally, tongue, earth-and-body-bound,
> servant of the other two, yearns to speak, to become
> one with the rebelling, silence-breaking rise, fall and holy
> wash of language.

Is this poem now complete? Does it move our conversation forward, or is it a mere prod at our outset, a hardly relevant artifact of our still-evolving journey together?

I'm content to remember the words of a very wise writing coach I once spent considerable time with: "Never judge your own writing." Amen.

Back to you, Keats, and "Ode to a Nightingale." You quote, "Was it a vision, or a waking dream? Do I wake or sleep?"

For Keats, the wonder comes from becoming both the questioner and the question; the human being. We live, hope, make mistakes, suffer. We may at four p.m. of a given day happen onto a revelation, an epiphany, that in the moment might claim to be life-changing.

Indeed, I sometimes picture Keats in the British Museum, viewing the Grecian urn. I want to see him exactly, feet, hands, posture, tilt of his head, and his eyes drinking in the artifact.

He does, after all, have a fine capacity to view something new, and then and there catch a ride, as he has it, on "the wings of poesy." In the museum, did he carry a notebook and pencil, then retreat to a seat, and, still viewing the urn, start his poem? Or, as with Wordsworth, was the experience later recalled in tranquility?

To stay with the human being, this upright animal, we can evoke Joyce's Leopold Bloom whom Joyce perches on the toilet at 4:30 on Bloomsday, his and our attention on his moving bowels.

Ah, as with Eliot, "the human engine, throbbing, waiting."

David

# 25. Deep Reading

## David,

T hanks for your latest thinking. Let me begin my response by expanding on a few of my previous remarks, as they appear to be directly related to some of your insights that I find particularly intriguing.

In a recent letter to you, I boldly suggested, drawing on the physicist Rovelli, that words might be considered creators of time rather than being entangled in the process of time (or perhaps even stuck in time). I indicated that I was conscious of the scandal of such an assertion and then went on with additional chutzpah to offer additional generalizations (or possible impossibilities) to help you think with me, or question me further, about matters of mutual concern. You have done that, and I want to continue along some of those lines now.

In Orthodox Jewish tradition, it can be said that the language of the Hebrew Bible does not primarily offer literary description but commands things to come into existence. That is part of its ethical force. I am talking here about what can be called God's language, though, not finite human language. "Let there be light," for example. But let me point out that the biblical text is also flowing with dialogue and stories as well. And it is purposely inscribed in a language that mortal human creatures can try to understand and interpret.

To claim that our human language commands such authority, or that we can fully understand such language, even Orthodox Jews would condemn as idolatry, a kind of blasphemy. In the

> The voice of scripture: not description but command

modern world, it is, of course, much more reasonable to assume, as most of us do, that the Bible was created by mortal and limited people (like us), and we might just as well leave it at that.

But I want to start there because I think it helps expand on some of the issues you have recently raised and calls up interesting questions about how we read and write today, and about what and why we read. I admit I have no ready answers, cannot bring it "home" (so to speak), but I find it important to expand the questions, explore them more deeply still. It is a question of emphasis, a way of inquiring about a sense of difference; not by any means an answer to anything, but a way of going forth, I might say. It is, in other words, not to determine necessarily what is "better," but to clarify the importance of difference along the path.

In this context, I might quickly add that the difference between the language of God and the language of the human is relevant here. There is a gap between the two, many thinkers claim, just as there is a gap between the divine and the human. At their best, poets often work within that gap, these critics often insist. The poets' work is always secondary; their creation, unlike the Creation, is a second order of things, many critics insist. I will return to some of the implications of this shortly, but, for the moment, I leave it as a question that calls for further probing.

Let me first take up some of the musical lines you have added now to your original poem.

I am struck by this parenthetical remark, for example:

> . . . protecting me from a final
> act of perfect, blinding sight.

I think that is exactly right in the framework you've created in your poem, and in a curious way it reminds me of some of our earlier conversations about silence and the Holocaust.

Paul Celan, perhaps the most important poet of the Holocaust, has a line that seems to resonate with yours here: "sightless / Your eye now goes silent into my eye."

And then your ending:

> . . . rebelling, silence breaking, rise,
> fall and holy wash of language.

Wonderful. And, as you suggest, we must then ask a further question: Is this "silent breaking," this "holy wash of language" (a stunning phrase) the end or the beginning, a return home or a going forth?

For the moment, I continue to resist the homecoming for the going forth, that is, the Greek for the Hebrew emphasis. As you suggest, in the end, we could claim it is both, but we are far from the end now. Even as second-level creators, we might say that writers do not so much take us home as engage in a process of separation, of disruption, of going forth, cutting away (as in circumcision), rather than a total unification, a complete gathering together (even a resurrection). To put it another way, we might say that, in Judaism, language does not so much search for meaning in an attempt to bring things together, to bring closure, but rather disrupts and separates, reminding us that "what is" is not necessarily "what can be," that even an apparent answer is only temporary, evoking another question.

I am thinking now in terms of what I would call great literature, not commercial literature or popular culture, not the kind of invention that leads back to "the same," that entertains us and distracts us, but the kind of creation that opens to difference, to new possibilities, not to necessity for all, but to freedom and justice for each.

Walter Benjamin reminds me of the kind of literature I have in mind when, in his masterful essay "The Storyteller," he contrasts news and information with genuine story—classic literature. The news is mere information which we consume quickly and forget in a short time. By contrast, great literature grows within us, is alive within us, becomes part of us as it flourishes. Most of what we get today is news, short-lived information, lacking even a half-life before it is consumed.

Mere "news" versus classic literature

By contrast, the poem or literary novel calls to us, and we respond to the call as it offers us a possibility. We enter into dialogue with it. Eventually, often after a long dialogue with it, the possibilities emerge as true to what we have encountered, what each of us has *experienced* through the reading and the discussion.

This is the process of what I would call deep reading, which always includes a need for waiting and for patience, leading even then not to total truth, but to a further questioning, a different horizon and an acknowledged, but not certain, possibility for something different, something otherwise. You see it, David, clearly in Keats, how through his poems he becomes the questioner and the question. This is the human being and the human experience, as you so well know.

When reading, then, we are at our best when we experience the doubleness of literary language, a language that allows us to feel the sensuous quality of the story / poem, its intimacy and desire, its somatic and emotional resonance, and, at the same time, to distance ourselves from the direct experience, to witness it, to reflect on it, but not to close it off or dismiss it.

I am reminded of Kafka in this context—his sense that reading and writing are crucial, that, for him at least, literature itself is life. Yet reading and writing also call for an endless deferral of judgment, much like life itself. With Kafka, we wait for the trial that never takes place, the castle that cannot be seen or found. It is always a going forth, without a return home, an arousal of anxiety and further desire, hoping, at its very best, to keep alive the impossible possibility, a flash glimpsed in the present. As Beckett, following in the wake of Kafka, says with a kind of absurd laughter, "Fail, fail again, fail better."

The no place: we cannot fully name it, yet we can experience it

Insofar as the no place (to return to that undefinable term) cannot be seen or fully named, we might nevertheless agree that it can occasionally be experienced as a kind of mystery in itself: in caesura, aporia, hesitation, stutter, the silence between the words, perhaps at moments in the midst of the voiceless or those speaking in tongues. Perhaps we sense this no place at a threshold just before judgment, in the free movement of indeterminacy, in directionless wandering, at the baffling crossroads in a Frost poem (such as "The Road Not Taken"). At times, it is the no place in between the writer and the reader. It seems available, but often not pursued—by the man from the country, for example, who sits outside the door but never enters the room in Kafka's "Before the Law." He sits at the threshold of the door of the law each day, the door opens to him and only to him, just as each book is open to each unique reader and only to that reader. Yet even at the threshold, it offers something for him, an enigmatic flash of something otherwise unseen.

We cannot expect language, especially since the Holocaust, to be totally clear; it is often barely legible, obscure, cloudy. We remain in exile, far from home. We might say, though, that it has always been this way. Rowan Martin, in his insightful book *The Edge of Words* says it well: "Language is not necessarily some kind of fallen distorting medium of activity; it is finite and historical, but not intrinsically corrupt. It can contextualize a silence which has not yet been said, or thinking which has not yet been thought." Through this silence might emerge a new "saying," a unique response to the other, even perhaps to the one who calls from no place.

At such moments, when we are summoned, we might find our freedom precisely because we then acknowledge that we are not alone, nor are we in control, as if we were sovereign by nature or identity. We can always hear the call, if we are willing; we can always relate to the other, if we dare. And so there are endless possibilities to go forth, to start over if we open to the possibility and responsibility implied.

Our response need not be what already is, the clichés and idle chatter of the moment, nor need it be related to bureaucratic apparatus or digital binaries or weighted down by material possessions. It might very well be something else, something otherwise, something different.

Literature at its best might be considered ethical in this context. It does not offer a categorical imperative (as Kant might), nor does it advocate for a single narrow perspective or position of sovereignty and control (as propaganda might). Instead, it calls to our desire to move onwards with the limited freedom given to us, a freedom that includes acknowledgment of the other and the responsibility to choose the "ought to" rather than the "is." If the news claims to tell us the way it is now, then important literature offers the possibility of how it could be otherwise, the freedom to glimpse how it might be. Perhaps it is not philosophic ontology (the chains of Parmenides), but ethics and psychology through poetry and narrative fiction that offer us the best hope for purpose and direction.

The ethic of literature: acknowledgment of the other

Walter Benjamin says that the source of literature in the days of enchantment was God, but now the source of literature is death. I am not sure I agree, but the point is well taken. It is perhaps a matter of faith and direction. We cannot describe God, nor the experience of our own death. In one sense, they are both "no place." With God and with our own death, isn't it a question of belief, an unexplained leap of faith (as Kierkegaard suggests)?

In *The Trial*, Kafka offers an excruciating scene in which K. looks up through a skylight in the dead of winter. It is as if he intuits (or hopes) that there is something else out there in the darkness, something sublime, perhaps a vast understanding. His hope is destroyed when he opens the skylight though and only mounds of snow fall on him, nothing else. But as I read that passage, there is hope there too. Perhaps not for Kafka at that moment of snowbound burial, but for the rest of us. This is what Kafka himself might have had in mind when he replied to Gershon Scholem's accusation that Kafka lacked all hope. "I have a lot of hope," Kafka replied. "Just not for us." Like Beckett, Kafka insists on the pain of laughter, the pain that allows him to carry on.

You ask, why do I say that we go forth like Abraham in the Bible rather than return home like Odysseus in *The Odyssey* or Jesus in the New Testament? As your last response to me eloquently demonstrated, we can find good examples both in Greek literature and in the New Testament for going forth. Given the paradoxical and contradictory nature of language itself, I agree that such categories are difficult, almost impossible, to fully sort out. But to clarify my position, allow me a couple of additional observations that I currently hold. Call them biases, if you like.

I think it is important in these difficult times to emphasize a sense of difference, a celebration of uniqueness, coupled with respect and dignity for all I quickly add, a feeling of connectivity and relationship with others, but not sameness. To return home, at least in one sense, too often suggests a return to "the same," to what supposedly was (or what is)—perhaps even to the stillness and beauty of Greek symmetry (as an end) or to the resurrection of Jesus into the divine body. But even in the most satisfying interpretation of the return, it can often signify an ending, a total satisfaction, a closure. Death, too, might be considered in this context as a return home to the final resting place. For me, the implication is then a "gathering together," a totality, a profound certainty. There is often something heavenly about it and a sense of perfection.

By contrast, I believe as human beings we remain in exile, wanderers, haunted by undecidability and indirection. Our hope is in our courage to start again, to separate so we can go forth, try again, loosen and untie the knots we have created. When Abram becomes Abraham, he has no home to return to; he is a wanderer with the courage to go forth, although he has no clear sense of where he is going and he cannot return to where he has been. This to me is an important moment in the Hebrew Bible, written before the Graeco-Roman era and before the New Testament (written in Greek). There have been moments, of course—the establishment of Solomon's Temple, the coming to America, the founding of Israel—that could be considered moments of returning home for the Jewish people. But the threat of destruction is ongoing, a perilous instability, never relieved, too often enacted. For me, it is not so much the eternal or the total or the timeless that make the difference, but the infinite and ongoing flow, history and time itself, the possibilities that lead to the making of a unique human life. And this, I think, is in the going forth more than in the return home.

To be human is to remain in exile

In your last letter, you ask an interesting question: Which came first, the diaspora or antisemitism? *Diaspora* is a Greek word, usually translated as "dispersion." The Hebrew word *galut* is usually translated as "exile." If we extend the meaning so we think of it as a going forth, a wandering, a homeless condition of sorts, a nomadic condition, a scattering, then we might even say that this kind of situation is ongoing from the time Adam and Eve are expelled from Eden, or the time Cain is marked and sent packing, or the scattering after the Tower of Babel falls, or the time of the Babylonian exile. In this context, I'd say exile probably precedes antisemitism, although antisemitism (that is, as "the Jewish question" or "the Jewish problem"—what should we do with the Jews?—leading to "the final solution") must have existed at least since the beginning of Judaism. In terms of how Greek culture and Christianity become the foundation for Western tradition, and how antisemitism manifests itself within this tradition, a recent book by David Nirenberg called *Anti-Judaism: The Western Tradition* offers the most insightful and disturbing explanation. I'd like to see it on every reading list.

Antisemitism and the condition of exile

I'd also recommend a new book by Emmanuel Acho and Noa Tishby called *Uncomfortable Conversations with a Jew*. In what Tisby calls a "quick semantic tangent," he insists that the words *Semite* and *Semitic* are actually totally wrong if used to describe any group of people. As he says, the word *Semitic* was first used in the late 1700s to describe all the languages of the Middle East and Africa that have linguistic similarities (Arabic, Hebrew, Aramaic, Amharic). But the speakers of those languages didn't have any other shared similarities of heritage or history. In other words, you could speak a Semitic language and still be anti-Judaism. Given the title of David Nirenberg's book, I bet the historian knows that, too.

Yes, the use and abuse of language makes the world go around. Spin the word and spin it again, and you will find much to consider.

When you say that much of our identity is dependent on what stories we inhabit from childhood, what stories, together with rituals and institutions, we are given and exposed to, you are spot on. Much of our belief has been shaped by family and friends, growing up in a particular community, living inside the stories that shape us as much as we shape them. This, too, is part of the dialogue that can make us human. But the Western tradition, so overwhelmingly Greek and Christian, has often created metanarratives that have dominated the beliefs and stories that are told, and in such a situation serious dialogue is often cut short. The Hebrew Bible becomes the Old Testament, scenes and characters in the Old Testament then become mere prefigurations of Jesus in the New Testament, the Jews become stubborn and incomplete in their beliefs, refusing to acknowledge "the good news" in the New Testament. To me, that is a context that deserves immediate attention and change in direction.

I remember when I was a young boy riding around with my father, looking at all the Christmas lights in the windows and on the lawns of homes, the colorful trees brightly celebrating the Christmas spirit in the parks and on the lamp posts downtown. I enjoyed seeing all that, but never felt a part of it, never thought this had much to do with the stories that made a difference to me.

By contrast, and in remembrance, I right now envision sitting with my father in the synagogue on the Jewish High Holidays. He is wearing his tallis around his shoulders and our Hebrew prayer books are opened. My father cannot read Hebrew, but his fingers move from right to left on the page, following the Hebrew text, as if it were a path for purpose and direction. I sit close to him, watching his hand move across the words. He looks over at me and smiles. I smile in response. It is not a nostalgic memory, a recollection from the distant past but, for me, a moment happening right now. His fingers moving forward across the words, his smile, his presence tell me that I have one unique precious life—onwards.

From your last letter, David, we also have your personal question—"Do I bear responsibility for antisemitism?" You might be interested to know that I ask the same question about myself.

The French philosopher Emmanuel Levinas might say that the key word in this question is "responsibility." For Levinas, we are all guilty (for everything), and so we are all up against the impossibility of achieving the perfection of ethical behavior. As Levinas (borrowing from Dostoevsky) likes to say, "We are all guilty, but I am more guilty than the rest." That "I" is a reference to Levinas himself, but also all of us, the "other" who is also "I." For Levinas, "the other" calls on the "I," and the I is then always responsible to respond to that call—to respond, in other words, to the ethical demand of the other. This too is always an incomplete exchange. We might think of it as the ethical demand for ongoing dialogue (call / response / call), on occasion perhaps genuine communication, but not completion. It is the unfinished work of mortal human beings.

To listen to the difference, to the uniqueness of each story, and to respond to it with our own uniqueness and our own precious difference is part of the challenge, perhaps the impossible challenge that I am considering here. As incomplete mortal human beings, we need each other, we are responsible for each other. And we are all guilty from the beginning, as the philosopher Levinas suggests. It is language, though, dialogue with the other, despite its near impossibility at times, that provides the near-impossible hope.

One another's stories: the responsibility shared by all

And perhaps even more impossible is that those who appear to have no story to tell—the homeless and the refugees, the wanderer and the strangers, those in exile and those in solitary confinement—are really now the ones who most deserve our attention.

But can a writer actually give voice to the voiceless? Can a writer tell the story of those who appear without a story to tell? Gayatri Spivak has made such an inquiry, asking, "Can the Subaltern speak?" It is a question fraught with difficulties. Even as witnesses, are we not implicated? And what about "the bare-naked man," the "muscleman" of Agamben? And those who have suffered severe trauma? Who speaks for them? Is it hubris or compassion, narcissism or obligation that drives the writer to dare to speak for all those who cannot speak? Is this the primary job of the writer, to listen to "the call" of the voiceless, to create language from the no place of those who appear voiceless?

Literature cannot be expected to provide the answers—nor should it—but it can provide us with a better understanding of the complexity of those questions. It can keep the discussion going.

I am reminded of the 1958 short story by Philip Roth called "Conversion of the Jews." Roth offers a glimpse of the difference I am talking about here. The idea of "the conversion of the Jews" has been expressed for a very long time as an answer to "the problem of the Jews" (or "the solution to the Jewish question"). But from a Jewish perspective, it is not, of course, a solution, but an impossibility. The Jewish martyrs have proven this again and again.

In the Roth story, Ozzie Freedman, a young and free-thinking Hebrew school student, challenges the narrow-minded Rabbi Binder by asking him difficult but serious questions about God. The Rabbi expects traditional blind faith; Ozzie expects American freedom to ask questions. For example, Ozzie wants to know why, if God is omnipotent, He couldn't create a virgin birth. Attempting to quiet Ozzie, Binder accidentally hits Ozzie in the nose. Blood dripping from Ozzie's nose, Ozzie runs in a panic to the roof of the Hebrew school building, while a crowd gathers below. Ozzie threatens to jump unless they all bow down and convert to Jesus. Ozzie then makes his point: you should not hit anyone for their opinions. He then, in a kind of cartoon dream scene, jumps from the roof into the halo of a net held by firemen.

The main point, as Ozzie makes clear, is not that Jews should, or ever will, convert, but that nobody should hit anyone for doubting the status quo, that is, for asking serious questions. For Roth, the satire is not only aimed at the narrow-minded Rabbi Binder but also at any reader who does not acknowledge "the Jewish difference." The lives of the Jews are not incomplete versions of the life of the complete mainstream Christians—that is, the "conversion of the Jews" is not a solution but a problem.

I mention this story in particular because I once taught it to a group of prisoners in a state facility. I didn't know it at the time, but the book group had been organized by three evangelical church members who invited me to facilitate one of the sessions. Near the end of our discussion that night, I asked the group what they thought Ozzie should do next, now that he was safely off the roof and everyone had probably returned to their normal routines. To my surprise, the general response from the group was that Ozzie still had a long way to go. Like the crowd below, Ozzie was still far from seriously acknowledging Jesus and far from breaking his stubborn and incomplete way of life. None of the Jews in the story could currently make it to heaven.

I left it at that. I suppose language at that moment was on the verge of collapse. To me, Roth was writing against this kind of American mainstream thinking as much as he was writing against the outworn thinking of Binder himself. He was doing what great literary writers often do—like Keats, Roth was both the questioner and the question. But I could not take it any further that sad day.

Let me end this letter now with another fictional midrash:

Stones can speak to us even today, but they are part of the original creation of the world by YHWH. At Mt. Sinai, the tablets are shaped and carved originally by YHWH from the stone, just as YHWH created the stone (like light) first with language but then, later, fashioned Adam out of the dust of the earth (perhaps stone itself). So we have the creation of stone, and the fashioning of tablets out of stone. The words, like fire, cut through the tablets / stone, perhaps first like the original words of creation ("Let there be light"), but then also inscribe words on the tablets, a fashioning of words, so to say, that cut through, from front to back, the stone tablets.

After Moses, angry when seeing the golden calf, breaks the tablets, they are again created, but, we might imagine, this time they are dictated to Moses, who inscribes them with YHWH looking on.

So, we now have a further demarcation of speech (oral) and writing (inscription).

The broken stone tablets in their scattered form are preserved in the Ark of the Covenant as well as in the copy finally presented to the Israelites. The broken stone tablets are a reminder of the shattering and wandering in the desert itself (and the diaspora in general); the copy of the tablets is a reminder of the covenant ongoing, but also its fragile and vulnerable nature, that is, "the gap" between what is and what ought to be (the possibility in the present and the not-yet of the future).

In the beginning is the end. And in the end is the beginning.

Bob

# 26. Homer, Kafka, and Literature at Its Best

Bob,

For this reply, I have two things in mind: first, reading vs. hearing, and second, where writing originates.

For the first, I had a cold last week and headed to my bookshelves. Making pretty much random choices, I came away with three books: Homer's *Iliad* (Robert Fagles's 1990 translation), Shakespeare's *Othello* (Folger paperback), and Arthur Koestler's *Darkness at Noon* (1967 hardback printing of 1941 Macmillan edition, now out of print).

I headed for our most comfortable couch for a pleasurable afternoon of reading, one I hoped would have relevance to our discussion, though not just sure how. To get started (even to prime the pump), I read again your recent missive where I had underlined some passages which have serious meaning for me. First:

> Literature at its best might be considered ethical in this context. . . . it calls to our desire to move onwards with the limited freedom given to us, a freedom that includes acknowledgment of the other and the responsibility to choose the "ought to" rather than the "is."

And then:

Those who appear to have no story to tell—the homeless and the refugees, the wanderer and the strangers, those in exile and those in solitary confinement—are really now the ones who most deserve our attention.

I am reminded of Kafka in this context—his sense that reading and writing are crucial, that for him at least, literature itself is life. Yet reading and writing also call for an endless deferral of judgment, much like life itself.

My first foray was into *The Iliad.* Not even out of the gate came the first lines in Fagles's preface, where he quotes Pope: "Homer makes us Hearers, and Virgil leaves us Readers." Pope, writes Fagles, thus "sets at odds the claims of an oral tradition and those of a literary one." So, speech or song over against reading.

Song and speech as literature

Suddenly I'm at an offshoot to aspects of our discussion that *reading* humanizes us. But what of listening? If folk music, particularly that of Bob Dylan, restores the oral tradition, how do we deal with it? Clearly, in 2016, the Nobel committee dealt with it head-on and awarded him the prize for literature, though Dylan wrote to be heard, and *is* heard, not read, for the most part. Indeed, his prose, *Chronicles* and, more lately, his *Philosophy of Modern Song* has nowhere near the quality of his songs.

In any event, we now absorb Homer as we do all the classics—by reading, unlike, say, with James Joyce, where every June 14 we can hear his *Ulysses* spoken, or, at least, read aloud. Given that, for one day, Joyce indeed makes us hearers, though (unlike Homer) he composed on paper, where, we might ask, does that fit into the oral tradition?

This of course begs the question of audiobooks, which I chalk up to convenience, not a deep-seated preference for hearing. That could be debated, of course.

Well, wanting very much to move from Fagles's preface to Homer himself, I chose (this being a war epic) to skip books 1 to 3—the preliminaries, the array of fighters, the talk in camps, the history of Helen and Paris, even the anger of Achilles—and went straight to book 4 to experience the poem at perhaps its most extreme, most tactile, and boldest: the battle itself:

130

Antilochus was the first to kill a Trojan captain,
tough on the front lines, Thalysias' son Echepolus.
Antilochus thrust first, speared the horsehair helmet
right at the ridge, and the bronze spearpoint lodged
in the man's forehead, smashing through his skull
and the dark came whirling down across his eyes—

Why is this so high-impact? Can any war photograph or movie equal it? I believe it is because language—everyday words—has been corralled and shaped to make us experience the turning of men into warriors and the actions they do. If there's any doubt that the epic lies anywhere but in the oral tradition, just live with that last line—a pure Homeric refrain, one used intermittently through the poem, similar to "dawn's rosy fingers" or "the wine-dark sea" in *The Odyssey*. That the dark comes "whirling," and specifically "across his eyes," posits the death experience in a whole new way, as only the warrior in death's grip could experience it, and a listener could appreciate it.

But let's remember, we no longer hear this poem. Since it was reduced to writing (sometime before the fifth century CE?), we read it. It is literature.

How does reading *The Iliad* square with our thinking? I would argue that the only way that I, as a modern antiwar reader, can truly encounter Homer fully is through the lens of an endless deferral of judgment, much like life itself. Thus freed of my own morality, I let the epic sweep over me, feeling deeply the Socratic awe and pity for these warriors, and the tale spun—chanted—by Homer.

But now to *Darkness at Noon*. This is pure literature with no roots in any oral tradition, though I suppose we might say that, as with all written novels and poems, ghosting somewhere behind the narrative is a campfire in a cave around which gather our ancestors, listening to a story.

So, its first line: "The cell door slammed behind Rubashov." Here we are readers, not hearers. And we are readers for 240 pages, accompanying Rubashov on his journey through pain, alienation, and hopelessness to his eventual small redemption—

survival. We are readers in a special sense, as the written word takes us to his cells, in his skin, and so, the closer we read, the less can we ever claim that we don't know what victimization by state police is.

In Rubashov we have a prime example of reading bringing us, in your words, face to face with "the homeless and the refugees, the wanderers and the strangers, those in exile and those in solitary confinement."

For *Othello*? Ah, Shakespeare and the art of the theater.

Playwrights write for the ear and the eye. It's spectacle after all that we yearn for when we walk into a theater. Multiply that manyfold for Greek or Roman playgoers. Did they ever expect to see a written version of *Madea* or *Amphitryon*? Did spectators in medieval England expect to see written versions of the mystery plays?

Bring on the Renaissance, though, and we have plays perhaps written for the eyes and ears, but written nevertheless, and comparatively easily rendered on paper—hence quartos published shortly after performances, and a First Folio just a few years after Shakespeare's death.

Works of literature—their enduring power, however they first appear, accounts for their remarkable longevity, generation after generation.

Now to a perhaps eccentric side trip I can't resist, as to where writing originates. How does an idea, and the conviction of its worth, enter the writer's mind? I'm prepared to say, purely for the sake of discussion, that the best ideas come not from the past, but from the future. Meaning that poets connect to future consciousness and channel who we will be then, and what readers will want.

Literature as dream, dream as prophecy

Here I want to set a writer's inspiration alongside his or her dreams. If dreams are prophecy, don't they indeed partake of—even live in—the future?

I'm thinking, for example, of Auden's "September 1, 1939":

> I and the public know
> What all schoolchildren learn,
> Those to whom evil is done
> Do evil in return.

But when do they learn it? In the future . . . either as children, or when they've moved into their full strength as adults.

Or Emily Dickinson's "I Taste a Liquor":

When Landlords turn the drunken Bee
Out of the Foxglove's door—
When Butterflies—renounce their drams—
I shall but drink the more!

She is positing her own actions not yet happened.

Or Eliot, concluding "Journey of the Magi": "I should be glad of another death."

Now, I accept that, in each case, I may be conflating the speaker's looking forward with the origin of the poem itself. But what if that's not the case?

What if "returning music" is in fact returning from a place similar to cloud storage, where computer data is stored nearly abstractly, where none of us has access except via distinct online portals? In other words, just previous to the act of writing, our minds slip to a place outside ourselves where our impulses and conceptual powers have previously journeyed (even if miniseconds before) and are now stored offsite. In this theory, the act of writing is a rush forward, retrieving our words, our music, from where they have already resided.

This theory posits the "nothingness" from which writing emerges as a kind of blank slate—an empty data file—which we ourselves first fill, then download from.

An implication is that when we feel strongly that we're channeling a past writer—Dylan Thomas, Yeats, Keats, John Donne, or Homer—we're actually downloading a copy from that writer's stored files, connecting with the past, but only insofar as that writer, in his or her real time, uploaded material forward, toward us. This casts in new light your idea of no place: a place that cannot be recovered or grasped, but which the poets (in particular) search for through history. It is the place that is and is not, the no place at the edge of creation.

A new light, yes, but it also refutes your lead premise that this material "cannot be recovered or grasped." *Au contraire*, it is a virtual place waiting to be made real by a poet reaching back to recover it by the act of reaching forward, and grasping it in two senses of the word.

Consider this in light of your further thought regarding the muse: the Greek Muses help the poets, inspire them to move close to this edge of creation. It is as if the poet, guided by the Muse, comes to a kind of boundary or bar that he leans across, listening intently for this nothingness, this silence which arouses him to respond with music and song.

The poet leans forward to mine the future

The difference being that the poet is leaning forward, to mine the future.

Well, I'll leave this theory for now. It certainly can't be proven, but neither, I think, can any other. I want to go on with observations that ring true regardless.

The music I heard by the pool—what of it?

> And so I return to music by the pool
> and watch the water's blue ripples
> kiss and kiss again the pool's concrete walkway.
>
> The sun passes overhead, eyes the pool,
> extends down transparent fingers to touch
> the ripples (a solar kiss or act of ownership?)
> till nightfall sends it packing.

I had never been to that pool, but for me it became all pools or bodies of water I had known. This was a return to water as a medium for pleasure, solace, and immersion. Six years ago, Sharon and I were traveling by boat from Rhodes to Turkey, and took a swim in the Mediterranean. Some decades previous, I remember walking in the sand of Cape Cod, entranced by the Atlantic, mind on connection, sex, love. Six or eight years before that, as a teenager, swimming at midnight in a pond outside of Jamestown, New York, eight, ten of us, mixed company, naked, music in our ears, full immersion all that mattered.

How do I know that nightfall "sends the sun packing"? It had done so then, as if in a dream, in a prayer answered.

Teenagers swimming in moonlight prompt me to move on to Romanticism, which surely needs our attention. Yet

134

considering Keats's and Shelley's poems, Wordsworth's *Prelude*, Coleridge's *Rime of the Ancient Mariner*, I'm given pause. These are brilliant and profound poems, of course, but I'd like to move the focus from content to intent.

If I access my inner romantic and pull it free of my psyche, I see my intent, which is to push emotion, and therefore expression, to a level I didn't expect. In other words, I do wish for completion, but also surprise—something beyond my own experience and even that of the reader.

Alternatively, if I access my classical instinct, I also wish for completion, but of a different sort—one firmly within the bounds of experience, and therefore, grounded in the acceptable.

When weighing the effect of favorite poets on these scales, things, I admit, get complicated. Those tending toward the classical: Homer, Dante, Eliot, Wallace Stevens, Ezra Pound, Sylvia Plath. In their work, they walk step by step to conclusions that feel preordained (even adjusting for modernists' penchant toward the obscure), as if we already know the outcomes that they take us to. This even though they allow us to experience awe and pity when we get there.

Romantics: Wordsworth, Keats and their contemporaries, but also, I would argue, Baudelaire, Yeats, Cummings, and Dylan Thomas. Their poems consciously push emotional limits such that we experience a sort of breathless wonder.

Joyce? I don't know. That he consciously brings epiphany into secular literature is telling: he wants us to realize the heretofore unrealizable. Is his intent, uniquely, something that classic and romantic writers share? And if so, is his novel then a bridge between the two?

Back to Dante, where I must take another tack. Rereading *The Divine Comedy* now, I believe I've changed since my last reading (20 years ago). Having nothing to do with classical vs. romantic, a whole new and intrusive issue arises for me. Having, I think, mellowed, and under the influence of Quakerism, and life itself, I am wholly disillusioned with the concept of retribution and punishment, in favor of a lenient justice.

But in *The Inferno*, Dante is invested in the punitive model. In fact, he rides it to a finish. Oh, and he does a tricky thing. Against

*Classical completion versus the breathless wonder of romanticism*

his will, and to his consternation, Dante the character is led by Virgil to the circles of hell. Indeed, Dante the character often sympathizes with sinners there and more often than not faints away when the experience becomes too intense. This poor fellow is close to being a victim himself. But we tend to not remark the obvious: that Dante the writer is anything but a victim or faint of heart. Indeed, he created the epic, chose the sinners, and their punishments, brought Virgil in, and invested each moment with horror and retribution. So, clever Dante gets to have things both ways.

Is *The Divine Comedy* in fact a comedy? To Dante, quite obviously, yes, in that it ends happily. But by, say, Shakespearean standards, it is not a comedy (perhaps at best a tragicomedy) because of the wall-to-wall suffering. In his comedies, Shakespeare lets nearly everyone off the hook, in that, by his enlightened view, we are all human and worthy of forgiveness. Enlightened Renaissance thinking vs. harsh medieval conviction.

Having invoked Shakespeare, just now I want to turn aside and consider the Fool in *King Lear*. Is this an accurate portrayal of what in fact Elizabethan court fools did? Lear's unconscious? A blend of both?

In any event, what the Fool accomplishes, along with undermining Lear's self-importance and folly, is to both broaden and deepen the scenes he's in. He broadens the restricted world view of the other characters through humor and often stinging satire. And he deepens the play, providing needed layering to our perceptions of characters' thought, behavior and expression. Added together, his presence is an off-ramp for theatre-goers and readers, giving us needed room to breathe and laugh as we're caught up in the ravaged, claustrophobic world of ancient Britain. Picture the play without the Fool, and we have a cruder, less nuanced work—one sadly lacking in one of the profound gifts Shakespeare gives us: the humanity at work in the most dire circumstances. Without the Fool, *King Lear* could well be the work of Aeschylus or Seneca or even John Webster, but not Shakespeare.

Who is Shakespeare? The Fool offers an essential clue

Thank you, Lear's Fool! Taken in the context of the Waxler / Beckman discussions, you are a gift to us: both a going out (broadening) and a coming back (deepening) all at once.

I don't want to finish without touching on other issues in your last, particularly in the realm of the oral tradition over against the written word. There is so much to explore here, and I revert to your book, *The Risk of Reading,* where your explorations are so thorough, with a profound and enlightened theme: The further we journey into ourselves through deep reading, the more we learn about who we are. I'll always plant my flag there, my friend. Yet I fear that the generation that follows us (and the one after that) may not so fully value self-knowledge, and therefore not recognize its absence as a core value. Please let me be wrong!

Ruminating on oral vs. written tradition, and the role of language, I'll share the following. It came not as a dream but a waking vision of sorts:

A man named Umbru stood at the mouth of a cave 150,000 years ago, looking down at a river and its long valley below. He was troubled that his people had lived long enough with simple utterances unequal to their thoughts, and he vowed not to step from that spot until he had spoken something new. Up from his throat came three words, one naming him, one connected to an action, one to a condition.

Without more thought, he said aloud: "I am here," surprised by the sounds his tongue made against his palate and the tears it nearly brought to his eyes.

Walking back into the cave to the twenty-five others who sat on logs around a fire, and who constituted his world, he repeated the words, and through hand gestures tried to show their meaning. After some quiet, his first-born son, Egree, aged fifteen, stood, bowed from the waist and said four words, the first being one they already had: "No, *we* are here."

At that moment, Umbru knew that Egree had the greater wisdom, and that his own days of leadership would soon be over.

David

# 27. Words Are Sound and Music

David,

T hanks for your most recent probing into the issues around the romantic vs. classical intent, reading vs. hearing, and where writing originates. I don't disagree with anything you have to say, but do feel compelled to give it a turn and then perhaps another turn after that one.

Quoting Pope: "Homer makes us Hearers, and Virgil leaves us Readers." Putting Gilgamesh aside, we might get Pope's point, interpreted by Fagles: Pope "sets at odds the claims of an oral tradition and those of a literary one." But that seems to be written by someone (Pope) who translated Homer as if Homer was Virgil, and Virgil was an urbane man of slick London letters like Pope himself. To put it another way, we might agree that hearing and reading are often a mixed art, probably going back to the time of Homer himself.

And what about Keats in this context, his reading Chapman's Homer? What a tangled web this is. Keats is awestruck with the emotional quality of the Chapman translation. I think Keats offers up what he reads by writing his sonnet. He could not have done that, though, unless he'd heard the music and sounds of Chapman's translation of Homer's Greek. As he says, he hears Chapman "speak out loud and bold." Is this reading or writing, hearing or speaking? I can imagine Keats up all night after his encounter with Chapman, pacing his room, speaking lines out loud as he writes them down, weaving his speaking with his writing, his listening with his reading. Probably pleased that he did not bother with Pope to begin with.

So, reading your last letter, I wonder in what sense the line "and the dark came whirling down across his eyes" must be epic and clearly part of the oral tradition? I agree that language outstrips any war photograph or movie in terms of high impact and emotional gravity. But why can't this line be heard from reading it? As you say, the line "posits the death experience in a whole new way, as only a warrior in death's grip could experience it." But why add that only a listener could fully experience it? Why not a reader? In the best novels and poetry today, I still hear clearly the voice of the writer; perhaps at the deepest level it is my unconscious voice, but it is a voice filled with sound and music. Sometimes that voice is even woven with the resonance of jazz clearly heard in the work of Baldwin ("Sonny's Blues") or Ralph Ellison (*Invisible Man*).

Literature that is resonant with music

And, by contrast, *Darkness at Noon*: "The cell door slammed behind Rubashov." An important story, as you put it, about victimization by state police, about those in exile and those in solitary confinement. We are with Rubashov from the very beginning. But, for me, and I bet for you too, someone who knows what that haunting clank of the metal door separating the free world from prison bars sounds like and means, that slamming of the cell door is not something that is just read at a distance, but resonates with outrage and horror; it's heard, passes through the ear to the human heart. It is a cry that ruptures all sense of well-being. So I need to ask: Is the experience of the relationship between us and Rubashov significantly different than our relationship with the Greek warrior with the blood from his smashed skull whirling down across his darkening eyes?

As you say, we know all this through writing, though, and without the scrolls and the scribes, the pen and the printing press, what we think of as the oral tradition might very well have been lost. Much of it has been. And, yes, there is what Barthes calls "the writerly style," literature not written to be heard but to be read. Of course, if there is a return to the oral tradition, as some suggest, the tradition of audio books or the lyrics and music of Dylan, there is also the new reading and writing found on computer screens, smart phones, social media. Images prevail, but words still can be found on the screens. But they are not print, not surrounded with the golden edges of a book (which is part of the enchantment that Keats finds in Chapman's "golden realm"). Instead of print, they are pixels that disappear quickly, like fragile words floating in air.

But what about where writing originates? Your idea here is striking and bold: "Poets connect to future consciousness . . . and channel who we will be then, and what readers will want. That returning music comes from a place similar to cloud storage." Although I instinctively resist metaphors and similes that draw attention to high tech, I am drawn to the doubleness of your idea that the act of writing is a crawl or rush forward, retrieving our words, our music, from where they have already resided. I am going to have to give this much more thought, although I am wondering who created that cloud storage to begin with and to what extent your sense of virtual reality is similar to the Romantic belief in the power of the imagination. Or is it the place of memory, the palace of the Muses? Perhaps we still live in mythic times?

Cloud storage—the Romantic imagination, or the palace of the Muses?

I also find your last comments on the music heard at the pool, and especially the way you weave the many dimensions of your own experiences into the fabric of the poem itself, especially interesting in terms of the power and importance of writing. The poem itself "sends the sun packing," I'd say; it is the enchantment of the moon (not the blinding white light of the sun) that allows us to dream and create, along with perhaps a kiss from the doe of dawn as we go forth near the break of day.

Perhaps words are sound and music connected to the speculum (the Latin for "mirror" or "reflector") which with the Romantic poets (according to someone like M. H. Abrams) gets transformed into a lamp? Is this the enchantment—the moon, not the sun; the indirect light illuminating the darkness?

Pope might be almost right when he focuses on the movement from the oral tradition to the written word, just as Marshall McLuhan was almost right when he focused on the changes from an oral culture to a print culture to a screen culture. And Owen Barfield was close to something important when he focused on how the "word" had changed as we moved from oral tradition to written tradition. But Charles Taylor in his inspiring book *The Secular Age* makes the crucial point that it is not really right to say that we have moved from a spiritual age to a secular age, as if history itself was linear, but preferable to see the ongoing mix of the secular and the spiritual—just as I'd say there is today an ongoing mix of oral and written tradition, hearing and reading, speaking and inscribing. And there is the speculum, the reflector or mirror become lamp, a reminder that our language (at least in its mortal and limited form) is a medium. It can be heard and it can be read, and it also becomes inspiration for what has not yet been written (the unwritten) and not yet been said (the unsaid—including that which cannot be said). We cannot think otherwise. Yet, I must add, "We can."

When I first experienced Allen Ginsberg's "Howl," I heard him shouting it out. He was on stage, near a microphone, with his bongo drums. "I saw the best minds of my generation destroyed by madness, staring hysterical naked . . ." It was not a song, but a cry. Later I read the poem in one of those small black-and-white pocketbooks put out by City Lights. Where did that cry come from? That's what I wondered then, and what I wonder now. It is a cry of isolation and forlornness, but also a cry for belonging and embrace. It's not that distant from "Call me Ishmael," a phrase now read out at the beginning of the festivities at the New Bedford Whaling Museum each year to celebrate the novel *Moby-Dick* with hundreds in the audience listening, just as they might be listening to *Ulysses*, that heavily written novel, on June 14 if they were in Dublin.

Can you hear this cry? *Eli, Eli, lema sabachthani.* Did it really happen, and does it really matter? "My God, My God, why have you forsaken me?" Did Jesus cry out at the ninth hour, in the middle of the afternoon, when all had grown dark, these words from the 22nd Psalm? Or did he sing the whole psalm, one that he must have known since childhood? Like most Jewish boys of the time, he knew them all by heart at a young age. Perhaps it was a psalm he had often sung with his mother, who was now standing with him near the cross. It begins in Hebrew, then follows with the language of the day, Aramaic, but we know it as the opening lines of Psalm 22. Perhaps the voice of Jesus is in that line, but usually when read, it is the music of David and the curve of his emotions that I sense, and perhaps the backstory of Queen Esther. I am the reader and the writer as I read and imagine it right now, the

The voice of Jesus echoing with the tones and stories of his Jewish forebears

141

listener bending forward, taking in the breath of the speaker, so I too might respond to his call.

In the broad sense, I embrace wholeheartedly your idea that poets connect to the future—not so much thinking about the distant past but the past flowing into the present and then the imagined future. Blake had grave reservations about Wordsworth for this reason, I think. We often claim that Wordsworth was the poet of memory, returning to the spots of time, recollecting in tranquility the sublime events of the past, similar to Proust much later looking into his teacup. Blake insisted on going forth, moving forward not backwards: revelation could be discovered at any moment, and that's why the work of creation continued onwards. His poem "London," for example, is a song, a song of experience, to be sung, but also etched on a copper plate, to be read, to be taken, one imagines, to heart, for now and for the future:

> I wander thro' each charter'd street,
> Near where the charter'd Thames does flow
> And mark in every face I meet
> Marks of weakness, marks of woe.

The wanderer, who is also the speaker and the singer, closes the poem by insisting that "most through midnight streets" he hears "the youthful harlot's curse." It is the song of the streets and the neighborhoods, the human cry of pain that he hears and responds to. But it is the language itself that I think Blake emphasizes here. As the wanderer says in the opening, he sees the marks of weakness, marks of woe, the silent anguish (and I would say, cry), the stuckness of the faces of the crowd that he passes. And what does he do? He "marks those marks," changes the reified noun, the frozen face, from a noun to a verb, brings the word to life again, gives it a flow (like the Thames itself) that will allow the word and act to come alive, that will help create possibility.

For Blake, it is clearly the imagination that inspires and aspires, not a soul distinct from the body. In this, perhaps, he is close to the more hesitant Coleridge, who became for the English Romantics, following Schlegel and the other radical Germans, a kind of spokesman for the imagination. For Coleridge, the "primary imagination was a repetition in the finite mind of the eternal act of creation in the infinite I AM." And then the secondary imagination, which is "an echo of the former co-existence with the conscious. It dissolves, diffuses, dissipates in order to recreate where this process is rendered impossible . . . it struggles to idealize and unify."

Blake never doubts the imagination as the creative power; unlike Coleridge, he does not say "recreate" nor does he hint at the impossible. Harold Bloom has called him "an apocalyptic humanist," an impossibility in itself but a unique one nevertheless. For Coleridge and the other Romantics, the flow of the imagination remains the breath of life, where Alph, the sacred river runs, but the word and world do not quite come together. The poet needs the reader to collaborate on a vision forward. The poet calls ("sounds the trumpet," as Shelley says), and it is the hope, if not the responsibility, of the listener to awaken to its intent and to take action.

The baffling complexity of Romanticism is its success and ironically its failure, its inevitable inability to fully complete the vision, leaving the poem incomplete and yet offering a glimpse of something else—like Coleridge hearing the knock on the door of the businessman from Porlock before the poem ("Kubla Khan" in this case) can be finished. Reading the poem in the present moment, we are enchanted by a vision and also experience a loss, a gap. Same with Wordsworth at Tintern Abbey, offering a sense of mourning for what has been lost and yet also creating timeless spots of vision arousing desire to move forward into the future.

*The poem in ruins, and the inevitable gap between what is and what can be*

This is the modern and post-modern condition: the exposure and acknowledgment of the gap between what is and what can be, the human and the divine, the limited and incomplete mortal and the limitless and total vision of immortality. It is possible, I suppose, that the no place may just be emptiness and that the bid to go forth may simply be an incomplete journey in need of a return home. If God (or the gods) can be thought of as the source of the Biblical text and the epic, and the world and the word are originally one, we now seem to have exchanged the source from God to death, and it is death, not God, that inspires us to speak and write in a fractured and fragmented world.

We need remembrance (not recall) to develop a story, to act it out, but must it always be a re-creation of a story, a mistaken and incomplete copy of the original? I have my doubts. "Make it new," Pound insists. And from a different angle, as philosopher Paul Ricouer notes, this might not be a failure in any case. Yes, we can say there is a gap between the original creation (the biblical narrative itself) and a later creation (literature as we know it). But this later creation raises questions too, important ones for sure. It offers a break, a rupture from the dominant plot of the mainstream culture, and so opens us to fiction (the "as if"), the possibilities, the imagination played on the blue guitar (as Wallace Stevens says).

As Maurice Blanchot has put it, literature is now a suggestion, not the steady white light of truth, but the twinkling disco lights that we think we might have seen. Literature gives us the gift of possibility.

In this regard, for me, literature still remains an opening, a place to begin. George Steiner puts it, more or less, like this: Reading demands our attention because it insists that we shift our orientation to something else. It makes an ethical demand to pay attention and to respond. It makes us realize we ought to do otherwise, although it does not tell us what to do. It breaks up our established ways of seeing and doing, takes us out of ourselves, so we can begin. It gives us hope and keeps us alive.

Has literature now become a birth rather than a creation, a struggle against death, eros vs. thanatos, desire pulling us to go forth and yet pushing us to return home? It is not so much the soul, but the breath that, along with language, God gives to the human, and we need that breath to be inspired and to aspire (to go forth). We need the senses and the body, and it is in that way that we need what we call memory, too. The trauma of birth and the trauma of death cannot be communicated. Nor can the beginning before the beginning and the end after the end—the no place that surrounds what we call our human and mortal life. Perhaps we can glimpse on occasion that other no place. But what seems clear is that literature, as you and I know it, can enhance empathy, bring the speaker and the listener closer together, encourage the dialogue between the reader and the writer. Perhaps without the power of creative language, there would be no empathy, no collaboration, only trauma and eternal darkness.

I would only ask a poet (or perhaps a kabbalist) this next question: Are the greatest poetry and the radiant rainbow analogous to each other?

Here is why I ask that, though I "tell it slant," as Emily Dickinson once put it:

Imagine a six-year-old standing on a dirt path in the middle of a small shtetl many years ago. The path runs through the village to the distant mountains. Standing on the path, the boy often wonders what is on the other side of the mountain. Fifty years later, he will be sitting with his family in America, listening to Kate Smith singing "When the moon comes over the mountain." We are not surprised that the song reminds him of that young boy in the shtetl.

But that is not the end of the story. Sometimes, when looking at that mountain, after a cloudburst, the young boy would see a rainbow above the mountain. It was radiant and filled with wonder and promise. But the boy never wonders about what is on the other side of the rainbow.

Why?

What is the difference between the perception of that mountain and the perception of that rainbow? Is it that the mountain does not need our help in its formation, because it is an "original" creation of God? By contrast, the boy helps to create the rainbow: the light and the raindrops require our mortal reflection to form the rainbow.

We cannot go over the rainbow, but we can go over the mountain. Why is that?

When that young boy looks at the distant mountain, he seems to wonder about an unknown possibility. He can go over the mountain, make the unknown known. And there will always be more to know. But what happens when he looks at the rainbow? He cannot go over the rainbow. It is impossible. It will always fade (withdraw) before he gets to it. Is this also the relationship between the reader and the text of great literature?

And, as always, there is something more to consider: "the beauty born of murmuring sound" as Wordsworth calls it, "the deep power of joy" when "we see into the life of things." I like to believe that that too is what that six-year-old felt when standing

The text as the ever-fading, ever-desired rainbow

on the dirt path in that shtetl so long ago, a boy under the rainbow, the sign of hope.

And that is also what our friend the poet Edwin Honig meant when he said about some of my poems in our *Echo Aonides* that he could hear, "ballads moving under them in the dark, refusing to surface, enjoying their own super-realistic firelights, clanging with streetcar fantasies of playful truth." As you put it in that collection of poems:

> Let us talk;
> Restless whispers in a restless night.

Language is where we live, not die, where we find the murmur of the breath which as readers we can activate: the transference of breath, we might call it. Let it be so.

So I continue to take up your most recent letter, the one you have sacrificed your voice to write, and I try to respond to that call, that which has no sound until I read it. And I try to connect my voice to it.

Like you, David, I love the Romantic poets. They are filled with surprise, offer endless inspiration, and I continue to turn to them for renewed hope and ongoing possibility. I think of the English Romantics as a more moderate version of the earlier German Romantic movement, and I think of them, together with the French Revolution and the arrival of the satanic mills (as Blake called the industrial centers created through the new technologies of the late eighteenth century) as a disruptive movement that celebrated the imagination and individual freedom, inclusivity and democratic possibility. As Abrams puts it, they transformed "the mirror" into "a lamp."

Of all the English poets, Blake possesses the strongest belief in the transforming power of the creative imagination, so strong, in my view, that he remains outside of any reasonable categorization of him. Harold Bloom calls Blake "an apocalyptic humanist," a phrase which suggests to me that Blake is beyond any grouping. Unique and irreplaceable, Blake has achieved his destiny.

The visionary poems of Coleridge—"Christabel," *The Ancient Mariner*, "Kubla Khan"—are rich with romantic sensibility and sublime desire (and have even loosely been compared to Dante's

146

*Divine Comedy—Inferno, Purgatorio, Paradiso*). Two of these poems, though, are incomplete, and we might, as readers, take the wide-open ending of *The Ancient Mariner* ("A sadder and a wiser man / He rose the morrow morn") as an invitation to go forth with the narrator and continue the ongoing tale, rather than as a warning to return home and coast along.

As for Wordsworth, the poet of remembrance, tranquility, and grief, I balance his "spots of time" with his profound sense of loss, and so note in our discussion here that a poem like "Tintern Abbey" often throws me to the site of ruins as if I am there in the present moment; and as magnificent as *The Prelude* is, it is at best the front porch of a mansion of epic proportions which, unfortunately, like the stately pleasure dome of Kubla Khan, never quite gets built. But yet, from Wordsworth, we also get the most sublime and visionary lines imaginable:

> . . . that blessed mood
> In which the burthen of the mystery,
> In which the heavy and weary weight
> Of all this unintelligible world
> Is lightened—that serene and blessed mood
> In which the affections gently lead us on
> Until the breath of this corporeal frame
> And even the motion of our human blood
> Almost suspended, we are laid asleep
> In body, and become a living soul:
> While with an eye made quiet by the power
> Of harmony, and the deep power of joy,
> We see into the life of things.

And with that "spot of time," we travel on.

The second generation of English Romantics, especially Shelley and Keats, also remain at the top of my list, but those two are clearly self-conscious not only in relation to themselves, but also in relation to the achievement and the failures of the previous generation. Byron is the exception, a negative romantic perhaps, but a strange split between an 18th-century satirist looking back to Pope, and a kind of Gothic existentialist looking at a time of horror and darkness, the world as a comic joke, a journey under the sign of an infinite jest.

By contrast, Shelley, Byron's good friend, is an intense but skeptical believer in the power of the imagination, I think. His best poem, "Mont Blanc," for example, comparable to Wordsworth's "Tintern Abbey," is an extraordinary expression of the power of the human imagination and its visionary possibilities. But Shelley has also confided that "the deep truth is imageless," and that puts any poet in an almost impossible situation. How can a poet balance the imageless truth against his own work as a poet? The skeptical Shelley can be heard loudly at the end of "Mont Blanc," which is certainly not a failure as a poem, but perhaps reflects a cautious poet stepping back from the abyss. Unlike Blake, who would rarely fall back (except perhaps to make a point as in the "Book of Thel"), Shelley, wisely perhaps, gives us another question:

If deep truth is imageless, where does that leave the poet?

> And what were thou, and earth, and stars, and sea,
> If to the human mind's imaginings
> Silence and solitude were vacancy?

Like Keats, as we have said in previous discussions, Shelley becomes the questioner and the question. Unlike someone like Conrad's Kurtz a century later, Shelley is not yet ready to step over that boundary into the silence and solitude of the heart of darkness, that place where tumultuous power makes what we thought was impossible possible: the horror that Kurtz sees and the horror to come. It will not be long, though, before Shelley takes the plunge.

We might say that with the English Romantics, we are well on our way to modernism and endless disruption, and, as you say, categories cannot hold for long. So, let me pause here again and think together with you about the categories classical and romantic, modernism and post-modernism.

There is bound to be confusion. (And we don't have to be a wise fool, the type we see in *King Lear*—and I will be commenting on him soon—to make that "prophecy of confusion.") We need abstract categories for clarity, I suppose, even if, ironically, they also lead to confusion. As the Fool puts it:

Then shall the realm of Albion
Come to great confusion:
Then comes the time, who lives to see't
That going shall be us'd with feet.

On these categories of classical and romantic, modernism and post-modernism, I find the approach of Charles Taylor in his brilliant book *A Secular Age* helpful. Taylor suggests that we think about modernism in two ways: as a broad and general category and as a more limited set of cultural categories (Enlightenment, Romantic, Victorian, Modern, and so on). I like this because it helps me clarify the complex and always confusing movement within the Western tradition from the belief in a stable and hierarchical world dominated by Athens (philosophy) and Jerusalem (Christianity) to the so-called secular world view, which emerges slowly in the 16th and early 17th centuries with the first modern philosopher, Descartes, and, according to Harold Bloom anyway, makes room through the work of Shakespeare for "the invention of the modern human."

I see this as a major disruption in consciousness that opens to remembrance and revision in the present moment and destabilizes classical thinking. We enter the multi-universe of ongoing and dynamic change, a variety of cultural modernisms that continue at least to the Holocaust. To me, this, admittedly generalized categorization helps provide a context for what comes to be called (by some critics) "literature" and its relation to human identity and the subjectivity of the self. It helps explain the rise of the novel, for example, as a cultural moment within the larger field of modernism. And helps me understand the kind of statement that Virginia Woolf can make—"On or about December 1910 human character changed"—as another significant mapping of a cultural moment of disruptive change from Victorian to 20th-century experience within the larger modernist field.

With this kind of context, I can see Yeats, a lover of Blake and the Romantics, finding an opening from the past—as the Romantics themselves did when looking to the sublime Milton and Shakespeare and further to Longinus—but then also claiming, in "The Second Coming," that "the center cannot hold," that essence has given way to chaotic existence, that God is dead. And what

From classic
to modern
via the
Romantics—
a vertiginous
journey

about Eliot? He insists on combining tradition with individual talent, but how many traditions are there really? Too many to count.
By the time Beckett arrives, the call becomes "Fail, fail again, fail
better." We are by then a long way from the Socratic imperative,
"Know thyself." The question itself has been reduced to fragments.
No longer, "Who am I?" but "Am I?" And with the ranting tongue
of the Nazis at the Wansee Conference on January 20, 1942, the
inhuman monster of the Final Solution emerges as the underside
of the so-called post-modern. The question is no longer "Is God
dead?" but "Is the human dead?" This is what Adorno was wrestling with. You and I, my friend (and language itself) have all been
put into question.

Yet I share your hope and love for literature and language, and,
as grim as some of this might sound, we are, in my view, still human beings, and there are still fragments of traditions that together with individual talent (which we all possess in our uniqueness) can make a difference. Adorno was right to insist on a time
for silence and disruption, but after that recognition we must still
uncover in the present moment what has been forgotten in the
midst of all the debris—if not for ourselves alone, then for the sake
of the corpses. Perhaps the goal is not any longer to "fail, fail again,
fail better," though, but simply to fail differently. Each in our own
unique and humble way.

Blake said, "Fear plus Hope equals Vision." I embrace that possibility even now. At moments, I even wonder if Philip Sidney's
Aristotelian defense of poetry as a way to teach, to delight, and to
move, could still have legitimate value. Can human actions be subject to ethical evaluation? Can Jerusalem and Athens be made one?
Does God or death sanction literature today? These are questions
that I continue to ponder despite the ongoing and intensifying
disruptions of the present moment. At times, I dare to believe—
and belief is necessary in such matters—that the gift of language,
even the act of naming, is a way, as you so eloquently put it, "to
experience awe and clarity."

But then, in a darker mood, I also wonder if the naming from
Adam onwards is more a diagnosis than a moment of joy—the
naming of the disease, the crime of life itself. If so, then, as it has
been said, philosophy is the cure, the preparation for death. The
cure often becomes worse than the disease in such a context.

Language becomes not the gift of awe and clarity, but a protective covering for the truth. As you say in your recent letter, "things I admit get complicated." The pen slowly slips from our hands, falling to the table (as the poet laureate Billy Collins once wrote).

But how can anyone not be inspired when reading Dante and Shakespeare? I am glad to know you are rereading both of those great writers now. Surely there is beauty and truth to be found there. Who dares to deny it?

You mention Dante as a man calling for the harsh punishment of lust and pride, and yet, like so many other poets, Dante is fraught with the shame of his own sins and pain. With you, I prefer a lenient justice, a superego with a light touch, a comedy that insists I take a close look at my own foolishness, a call that makes me respond by laughing at my own limitations and absurdity. Dante has written a divine comedy, sublime and beautiful, but there is little comedy here. And so, like you, I, too, note that Dante often appears to revel in the punishment itself. Perhaps, though, there is a little bit of Sade in all of us? And if we are all guilty (as Dostoevsky and Camus suggest), then how can we rationalize such judgment of others? And how can we forgive ourselves? I have never been comfortable punishing others, thinking that somehow the others are bad and I am good, that the other is the monster. I, too, am responsible for the crime (whatever it might be). Like Kafka, I'd like to know.

I cannot forget Virgil, though, a genius for naming, a poet who celebrates with the beauty of language the possibilities and glory of Rome (and Dante, too, celebrating the wonder of Florence as well). But yet, as Dante's guide, Virgil cannot bring Dante beyond the gates of heaven; only Beatrice can guide him across that threshold. And then what remains for Dante? Only a gazing at his true love at a distance, never to embrace her again. Orpheus would understand, I am sure.

Language remains our best hope, but only if we have the courage to believe in it, and perhaps the humility to admit its limitations. But what are its limitations? On a bright sunny day, I am sure that the word and the world are one; or to put it the other way round, that the world would collapse if the word disappeared.

With all its limitations, language remains our best hope

Yet we find Nimrod in the ninth circle of hell, one of the giants of ice: Nimrod who insisted that the Tower of Babel be built so he

151

could make a name for himself. Is this the corruption of language getting the punishment it deserves? As I have suggested many times now, the result of Nimrod's idolatry sends language itself into exile, a disruption that perhaps only poets and prophets, visionaries and wise fools, will dedicate their lives to repair.

David, I am glad to hear that you are rereading *King Lear*, my favorite Shakespeare play. Harold Bloom, unfortunately, judges the play to be, at its core, nihilistic, but, unlike you, he seems to dismiss what the audience can see and experience despite the central tragedy itself. I am thinking, for example, of the virtue of Cordelia's love, despite it all, and the wisdom and loyalty of the Fool, his lack of pretense. As you say, the Fool both broadens and deepens the play, and so helps us as readers to broaden and deepen ourselves. "In deep is far out."

But I cannot agree that your assessment of King Lear indicates a journey home, a return, but rather an inspiration to go forth and continue on. Even in your story about Umbru and Egree, I see that sense of going forth. In their case, I experience a passage from one generation to the next, generation hopefully becoming regeneration. Such transition, such passage, broadens and deepens, I agree. But it is a unique moment, as all such passages are, a moment in which the word remains in exile, the world hangs on a thread. I call that thread the breath that grants us ongoing desire, a nagging intensity to move forward.

The same holds true for the Fool in *Lear*. Yes, he certainly broadens and deepens the experience of the play for us. He allows us, as the audience, "to smell out and to spy into." More fully, and more disturbingly than Umbru or Egree, the Fool grants us his breath, a thin thread to go forth with.

Sometimes I like to hope, as you do, that the Fool is actually saying, "Let me teach you something"—that is, let me delight you with entertainment and song, let me move you to reasonable moral action, to the Aristotelean middle way, to Greek virtue. Like Lear, I, too, have a nose in the middle of my face, and eyes on either side. Even if Lear is not moved, perhaps the thin thread that the Fool offers up will still be found by others. Is it possible?

What happened to the Fool? Lear believes he was hanged, but he would also like to dream that Cordelia lives on. Most likely, the Fool was lost in the storm on the heath. He never returns home, but disappears from the play and perhaps from history itself. If he ever did exist, some might say it was a very long time ago. He seems to have died in the mythic consciousness of ancient Albion, long before Merlin and the magicians. Yet actors and audiences, Shakespeare and his readers, have all breathed new life into this corpse. He is remembered today. Not yesterday, but in the present moment. Not recollected from the past, but remembered in the present, as if he sits near me as I read *King Lear* today.

Permit me to introduce a different bit of magic, a poem you recently sent me. It is clearly your voice I hear. And for some unknown reason, it connects me today with an episode from our days at Brown, an episode that marks our friendship forever and even helps me forgive others who might have been involved.

We were four roommates in those days, living on Hope Street near the college campus: You and I, Ivan Cohen, and Harry Roy. We agreed to buy together a sharp-looking '49 maroon Plymouth with four-speed shift on the floor. We shared the exorbitant cost: $20 per person.

Tired of Brown, I yearned for further adventure. Perhaps material for a book, Jack Kerouac was on my mind. I headed to New Orleans through the deep South, a dangerous place in those days for young Northerners with long hair. At two in the morning, a sleepy Alabama cop stopped the car on the road. "I wouldn't have stopped you, but your car was making so much noise it woke me up," he said with a smile. "I'm going to have to put you in jail overnight and check your background and record. You look like one of those agitators."

In the jail cell that night, the cop brought me a photograph of a group of young Northerners under suspicion. He pointed to one of them and said, "This fellow looks a lot like you." He left without saying anything more.

In the cell next to mine, though, was a Black man playing blues on his harmonica. I responded by reciting some Blake poems and then he played some more blues. Back and forth. We were talking to each other for about an hour with music and poetry, creating a bond between us that will never be forgotten.

Blake and the blues

The next morning, the boys at Brown were up early and apparently knew I had taken the car. Harry Roy had notified the police, and he wanted me arrested. It was you, David, who saved me, though. Your voice, unheard by me at the time, echoes to this day. You convinced the others to back off, to let me continue my journey onwards.

"We're going to let you off before you have to go before a judge," a generous police officer told me. "But you better get out of town as fast as possible. There are KKK members already gathering at the local coffee shop eager to see you. These boys are proud and dangerous."

The car was no longer working, but, freed, I headed out of Opelika, Alabama, that day, hitchhiking to New Orleans.

David, I'll always believe it was that voice of yours, the poet in motion, that saved me from disaster.

I hear that voice mingled with all your other voices whenever you speak. Thank goodness for that. And, yes, your poem "Chair," in a very different style and context, also helps me to forgive Harry Roy ( even if he seems to have been a "betrayer"):

### chair

arms
      inanimate

you
    receive
      then
          release
            me

to receive
    another
and
    another

betrayer

As a "betrayer," the chair, if it were human and animate, might be a strong candidate for Dante's ninth circle, the coldest and darkest place in hell, reserved for Iscariot, Brutus, Cassius, the ultimate examples of betrayal. But, of course, as a reader of your poem, I seek no revenge. In fact, I think of the poem at first as if it were a fragment jotted down in a notebook. To read in it anything more than that is to overread it. It is a joke of sorts.

But when I read the poem, I rock back and forth with the chair and slowly become one with it. Only at the end (with the word "betrayer" hanging there) am I jolted ahead and pleasurably surprised.

This small poem has wit and humor, disrupting me with its reversal at the end, evoking laughter at the human condition. It is a good joke.

Yet there is also something else that appears here. The poem is not exactly what I might have thought it was at first. Perhaps even its opposite.

I see the words of the poem do not point outwards from themselves towards an inanimate chair. Instead, the words and the imagined object (the chair) become one as the words open inward for me (the reader). So I enter the poem again, go forth into it. The chair, in other words, is not seen through the words. It is experienced, as the poet too experiences it in his own way, within the words themselves. The "outside" becomes the "inside" as the chair emerges within the words and takes on its own uniqueness. The rhythm and voice of the poem moves toward revelation, but stops short, demanding disappearance instead.

Have I been fooled by the trick of naming? The chair has betrayed both the poet and the reader. It is as if the poet and the reader, you and I, David, become something else. Having experienced the words of the poem, the rhythm of the language, the world that surrounds us, we now become interpreters. The chair has again returned to the outside, and we can step back and contemplate it together, question it, from a distance. Your voice in the poem invites me to friendship.

Through the gift of language, the poem promises more than it knows, more than we thought it said. And, is the chair, we might ask, being separate from us, now an enemy or a friend? I ask, does it only receive others and then throw them off, or does it also call to us, as an animated part of our lives? Has your poetic rendering of language again opened a disruption that offers through language new possibilities? Despite its imposed title, "Chair" is closer to a verb than a noun. It is not a name, but an event of naming. It makes a difference.

We should not expect too much. In terms of poetry, Celan might have had it right when he said a poem is *en route*, it never arrives. As he put it in his Bremen Lecture:

> For the poem does not stand outside time. True, it claims the infinite and tries to reach across time—but across not above.

For Celan, every meeting is a missed meeting, but perhaps one day it will happen. The poem sent out in a jar across the ocean might yet wash up on the shore of some remote island.

Utterance as a verb, not a noun

In a similar context, Wittgenstein claimed that the truth is not to be found in the said, in the "name itself," but in the saying, in the event of naming. For Wittgenstein, what he calls "utterance" is an act, not a name; a verb, in other words, not a noun. Through "utterance," the word opens our breathing to keep life in play. We cannot know the mysterious truth that we seek, but we can acknowledge the breath that fuels the desire to continue on. As Walter Benjamin says, we close the book when the hero dies, but his death warms us, the readers, and gives us breath and courage.

Yet, I have to add that "Chair" also invites me to consider another kind of question: Why do we write, if we know that the promise of writing, like the initial promise of the chair, like the promise of life itself, will eventually betray all of us? I think about our previous discussions regarding the fundamental difference between the Western tradition (dominated by Greek and Christian) and the remnants of the Jewish tradition (which could be considered the third pillar of Western consciousness but in reality lives on despite ongoing attempts to destroy it). Within the Hebrew Bible, as I read it, the letters and words are open and polysemous, creating infinite possibilities through time. It is as if hundreds of voices can be heard, purposely destabilizing and disrupting any sense of a final answer. By contrast, the Greek and Christian traditions tend toward the image, stabilization through the visible. We work to gather all together, until this and that become one.

Again, Wittgenstein is helpful. Speaking about philosophy, he says, "a picture held us together," and that is the problem with philosophy. It started with an acceptable picture of what is, and then it became the foundation for everything else. For Wittgenstein this was a wrong assumption from the beginning. He clearly prefers poetry to philosophy; words, the breath and verb, free us through movement, rhythm, sound, utterance. It is the "saying" not the "said," (as Emmanuel Levinas would also put it) that keeps us alive and grants us hope.

Poetry versus philosophy: the saying versus the said

I will stop this response shortly. But before I do, I want once more to move sideways, just briefly, to your important point about the separation and connection between the Classic and Romantic traditions. Such categorization is crucial and leads, as I think we both agree, to contradictions, confusion, even breakdowns in logic. Categorization is necessary, but it is an illusion. Poetry and fiction come much closer to the truth than any categorization can possibly do—in part, because they insist on contradiction and messiness, disruption and ambiguity. Through literature and language, we are offered our best hope. Our cultural age, call it post-modern for the time being, has hidden deep within its bowels the texts of previous ages, and each age is filled with disruptions which open new discoveries forgotten and yet to be. Through the depths of literature, we can still create new wonders discovered from the past opening to the present, and project them towards the future. Through literature, we find the questions we need, if not the answers we want.

Literature continually contradicts itself. But this is all for the good. As your good friend Walt Whitman put it, "Do I contradict myself? Very well then, I contradict myself." Literature in its flow, like the breath and the river of life, might yet open us to what is and what is not. We can be that young six-year-old journeying over the mountain and, yes, perhaps even standing under the rainbow, the sign of hope and freedom, even beyond necessity. Pace Parmenides.

Bob

# 28. Chaos in the Bible and Shakespeare's Tragedies

Bob,

"Fear plus Hope equals Vision."—William Blake

"May we find the questions we need, if not the answers we want."—Bob Waxler

Harold Bloom does indeed judge *King Lear* as nihilistic.

Is it? Before addressing that, I'm inclined to ask, what of Shakespeare's other tragedies? A common aspect of *Macbeth, Othello, Hamlet, Romeo and Juliet*, and *Julius Caesar* is that, however bloody the ends and dire the destiny of their characters, each play's final act restores order (or establishes a new one), and thus undoes nihilism.

Is order restored at the end of *King Lear*? The last lines are not ones of hope. Edgar: "We that are young / Shall never see so much, nor live so long." I think Samuel Beckett derives from *Lear* in knowing, with *Lear*, a bleak, unrelenting darkness (albeit, with Beckett, laced with humor).

An allied concept to nihilism, apt to Shakespeare, is, of course, chaos. In the middle of his play, Othello invokes chaos and, doing so, opens a path to nihilism: Regarding Desdemona, he says, "If she stops loving me, chaos is come again." I've always wondered about the "again" in that line. Exploring our current subject gives me a chance to think about it. Why doesn't the line end simply with "chaos is come"? The "again" calls up something primal that existed in the deep past, so is pre-modern, pre-Renaissance, pre-Christian, pre-Hebrew, pre-Greek, in a way that the line would be otherwise free of. But with that one word, Othello shows a lurking threat that his soul knows and fears. With Shakespeare's choice to provide the "again," I infer that he knew that we foundationally come from chaos and, if we're fortunate enough to live in an enlightened age, as he did, and if we behave reasonably well, chaos is temporarily at bay, yet always lurking and ready to open its jaws as a result of our actions or inactions, individually or culturally.

Chaos—the source of everything, only temporarily at bay

Let us follow his lead.

The word *chaos* appears a dozen times in the Bible. Perhaps its most salient appearance is in the Book of Isaiah:

> For this is what the Lord says, who created the heavens. He is God, and the one who formed the earth and made it, and he is the one who established it; he didn't create it for chaos, but formed it to be inhabited.

Then this remarkable add-on, sans segue, changing from third person to first: "I am the Lord and there is no other."

Aren't the implications here far-reaching? Chaos, by this cosmology, is absence of order, and order is a gift of the divine. To invoke the secular, in the OED, chaos is "the first state of the universe." Then what is order? In Isaiah, it's God's creation, whose final word is that of an absolute ruler: "I am the Lord and there is no other." Is the implication that to doubt the Lord, or worse, to fail to obey him, is to invite chaos? No, *is* chaos? Christian literature banks on this, from Dante's *Commedia* to Eliot's "Ash Wednesday":

> Because I do not hope to know
> Because I do not think
> There, where trees flower, and springs flow . . . there is nothing again.

"Nothing again"! Chaos and nihilism joined.

159

What, then, is nihilism? With Latin *nihil* translating as "nothing," it is of course, nothingness. Or, more accurately, being an "ism," a belief in the prevailing reality of nothingness. It is more modern and radical than chaos. Not for nothing (no pun intended) did Sartre oppose it to "Being" in his book's title. A common definition (OED) is "a negative doctrine in religion," and it seems to have first appeared in German thinking in the early 1800s, then spread eastward to be popularized by Turgenev in *Fathers and Sons* (1862). It evolved, with Nietzsche, as "no objective order or structure in the world except what we give it." (America avoided it for another 100 years or so.)

Did Lear, at the end, see no order or structure in his life? Could he give it none? Surely he had undercut the structure of his world in the first scene, when he banished Kent who loved him and was loyal to him, and when he rejected the one he loved most, Cordelia. Does this make the play nihilistic, or just Lear himself? Here we come up against the essence of drama, where a main character doesn't just adopt a world view, he *is* a world view. We are conditioned, to our peril, by religion and culture, to conflate these two things, as does the writer of Isaiah, whose Lord (the hero of his epic) claims that he not only formed the universe but that he is the only Lord, the only hero of the epic: He *is* the universe.

Nihilism embodied by Lear himself

By way of refutation of all this, and as an antidote to it, we moderns need only stay true to what we know of the universe today, thanks not only to astronomy as it started with Galileo, but to contemporary images sent back by the James Webb Space Telescope: the universe is enormously more vast and more populated by stars and galaxies than any Iron Age writer could have known or imagined. And far from being in the center of it, we inhabit a tiny sphere in a remote neighborhood.

Is that chaos out there, scattered in all directions for billions of light years? Or order?

The answer is in the eye of the beholder, and their mind. (Oh how I hate using the plural pronoun here, but how else avoid the awkward him / her construct? What do linguists say about this now nearly ubiquitous usage?)

You have rightly asked, what happens to the Fool in *King Lear*? And you posit that Lear believes he was hanged, and would like to dream that Cordelia lives on. If Lear needs to ask about the fates of these two people, isn't that proof of his mind reaching for order?

As readers of the play, we accept Lear's comment on the Fool—that he's dead, and that "I killed the man who hung him," allowing him one more kingly act of murder without judge or jury. Lear still knows he's king and above the law in this regard. And so, hasn't he imposed order on his life, and therefore his world?

As for Cordelia, we see her die—almost! Lear thinks he sees her breath at the end: "Look! her lips! Look there. Look there." Does he see her breath? Does she survive? (Nineteenth-century productions of the play certainly went down that route.) But no, we accept her death. She dies for filial love. She represents balanced filial love tempered with sanity—she loves her father sanely, i.e., precisely to the extent that a rational nature dictates. Isn't her death acceptable ultimately only to an ordered mind, where cause and effect still hold sway? The play dramatizes Lear's madness, his personal disorder, visited upon his child. Is this chaos or nihilism? Neither—it's order, though of a dark nature.

Your ruminations on "Chair"—a reader finding a way into a poem—fascinate and stimulate me. That I am the poet intensifies two experiences for me: first, taking in your reading and appreciating your thinking as it proceeds; then, looking back at the poem with new eyes, in the penumbra of your thought. Recalling, I suppose, in tranquility, to allow an application of Wordsworth. Many aspects of your comments stay with me, and I will dwell on only one—your discovery of the poem's humor. I recall that in arriving at the final word, "betrayer," and not knowing till then that that's where the poem was headed, I was gripped by a sly wryness (or wry slyness) impossible to resist. Ending on that word amused me as much in itself as in anticipating how it would land for a reader, whose expectations, like mine, up to then, might be wholly elsewhere.

I suppose much of the charge is in the chair's being inanimate in the early going, but achieving animation of a sort and, to that extent, acting human. Do any other things, animate or otherwise, commit betrayal? I'd say no, only humans (just as only we love, hate, yearn, and plot revenge). That in the poem a chair joins us in our humanness creates the scintilla of amusement.

Invoking Paul Celan here is most apt, inviting us to ponder a poem's journey, and his conviction that it never arrives, but only travels toward . . . what? One of many possible endings? Or no ending at all?

Here I confront the ups and downs of crafting a poem, and the fragility of a poet's consciousness, versus a reader's need to paper over any such fragility in order not only to fully appreciate the poem, but to experience it as a gift, something to tuck away in his own consciousness, and to reap its fruits.

It would be the same thing if you were the poet, and I the reader.

Deep reading is impossible without empathy

You, with Steiner, find reading to be an ethical act. And *you* see it as an empathetic one—an idea I like a great deal. Do tyrants read deeply? Do rapists and murderers? It's tempting to say, "Only if they have forgiven themselves their inhumanity."

Can one imagine Hitler reading Thomas Mann? Stalin reading Tolstoy? Putin reading Akhmatova? Trump reading James Baldwin? I think not, and not because of ideological differences, but, I venture, because a tyrant cannot read deeply until undergoing a most profound metamorphosis where self-forgiveness becomes the lubricant to profound change, and empathy replaces rage. And what tyrant ever ventured there?

You end your last with an ironic tribute to Parmenides, and by extension, the philosophy of ontology. The fact that early thinkers were parsing the here-and-now and the perpetual; the abstract and concrete; what may be with what must be, is surely a tribute to their cultures. When, in pre-Christian Greece, did education and discourse advance to such a level? I would like to see a timeline from say, 800 BCE through 400 CE to the Renaissance, with "crude thinking" at the left, "sophistication" at the right, and everything in between.

Furthermore, if an individual's development replicates that of a culture, then how would that individual proceed along that same timeline? Is an eight-year-old's thinking crude? Is a sixteen-year-old's less so? Is a twenty-year old on the path to sophistication? A thirty-year old fully arrived? Then what of a seventy-year-old? An eighty-year-old? If someone takes good care of their self and their mind remains sharp, might the sophistication of their thinking be in the stratosphere?

I think so, though showing it depends on performance—an octogenarian, say, demonstrating excellence through writing, art, musical composition, mathematics, or chess. An advanced age may inhibit expression of this, as may motivation. So do we have thousands of older people trapped with their sophisticated thoughts locked inside?

Acknowledging that my setup and assumptions here may themselves be crude, and inviting correction for that, still, how to view contemporary Americans' place on that timeline? As a culture, are we yet on the positive side of sophisticated thinking? Or backtracking?

I ask because I think one can argue that (reverting to one of our pervading themes), as we move away from print and toward full dominance of television, film, and electronic communication, we are, as a nation, a culture, entering a new era of crudeness, regardless of age. If so, will we increasingly devalue sophistication, preferring speed and shallowness? What does such shallowness look like? I'd submit that its earmarks are reckless conclusions, lack of grounding in objective discourse, reliance on emotion disconnected from reflection, and going into action (political, especially) free of insight and the ability to discern cause and effect.

A new era of crudeness?

## David

# 29. Evolution and Progress

David,

I cannot disagree with your comments on the development of the human mind. Nor can I disagree with your thoughtful comments on *King Lear*, especially recalling your hard work as a performing stage actor in our days at Brown and your unique experiences as a member of the National Shakespeare Theater Company. Your take on American contemporary culture, its shallowness and its reckless obsession with "the screen," is something that I fully share with you. But we have our differences, which demand ongoing dialogue and connectivity.

For example, when you suggest the idea of evolutionary development from a crude brain to a sophisticated brain, I certainly agree that the difference between other animals and the human is that we appear to be the rational animal, but, of course, as humans, we are also often unreasonable. And to make matters more complicated, some of the other animals are bigger than us, physically stronger, and seem often to know better than we do when to fight and when to take flight. Perhaps our only advantage is having a complex language; it helps us to create the illusion of reason, and to mitigate troubling instincts and drives. But language always overflows its boundaries; like human life itself, it is messy and often unreasonable.

And, yes, what we might think of as crude animal instincts often seem to serve survival needs better than our poor attempts to be reflective or reasonable. I think, for example, of Jack London's "To Build a Fire." A story about a man and his dog in the cold Yukon wilderness. The man attempts to think his way through the deadly challenges his surroundings present, but his choices are marked by foolishness and ultimate failure. By contrast, the dog survives through a different process of thinking, one we might call instinct. At the end of the story, the dog trots up the trail in the direction of home. The man falls silent, into sleep and death in the wild.

So if you are making an argument for evolution as some kind of progress, I am more likely to say, not evolution but difference. "The child is father of the man," as Wordsworth put it. The innocence of childhood, according to Blake anyway, is different than the experience of adulthood. But there is, to me, not so much a sense of progress here, but rather a sense of difference.

I think about our own relationship and our deep friendship— at Brown, cleaving to the edge of the other through literature and language, but also by a common interest in freedom and true democracy, and yes, in young women on and off the campus. I don't remember any serious disputes between us, except perhaps over who was going to wash the dishes or clean the living room. And here we are today, sixty or so years later, writing letters to each other about literature and language, still sharing our common interest in freedom and democracy. We are old men now, though, both married to outstanding women who care for us as we care for them. Perhaps we could say that's progress. It certainly marks out a difference.

*Difference, but not progress*

If you press the issue, I might suggest, jokingly—as debaters on evolution in the 19th century did—that perhaps some people evolved from apes, while others came directly through Adam. But, in my dream world, I'll take the side of the mythic history of Adam, who it has been said wrote the Book of Creation. I like that notion, because it suggests that there was literature and language from the beginning.

I do agree that the science of medicine seems to have advanced from its crude beginnings to modern sophistication. But then the cure is often worse than the disease itself, and I see no sign that we have come close to curing death, the terminal illness that we are all born with. By contrast to the progress of medicine, I can make no argument that literature or the humanities in general have evolved to a higher state, nor has democracy for that matter. And, of course, it is worth pointing out that Socrates did not own or need a smart phone—and I am thankful for that.

I am also taken by your linking *King Lear* with an insightful consideration of chaos and nihilism. I like your point that chaos is the ally of nihilism and that the phrase "chaos again" in the play helps define the deeper meaning of the play (and, by implication, tragedy in general). But again something sets me wondering, making me question the nature of tragedy itself and the relationship not only between chaos and nihilism but between pain and death. In other words, my good friend, I have my differences with you on some of these matters.

The narrow view of tragedy embraced by Aristotle

For example, I don't think we can fully trust Aristotle on the topic of tragedy. We are indebted to his splendid defense of tragedy (and literature), a kind of response to the mixed call of Plato on the value of literature. But Aristotle's apparent choice of *Oedipus* as a model for his theory of tragedy seems unfair to begin with. It serves well the Aristotelian sense of reason, and lends the play an unsurpassed dignity and power, but why not choose a different play, say, Sophocles' *Philoctetes*? Here is a play that does not yield to pain and suffering, that lacks the kind of symmetry of structure that Aristotle rightly finds in *Oedipus*, and that leaves even a susceptible audience short of any catharsis (from my perspective anyway). To me, there is something of "the howl" that rings through all tragedy, from the howl of Oedipus to the howl of King Lear ("Howl, howl, howl, howl!—O you are men of stones"), but the howl of pain in *Philoctetes* lingers; it cannot be contained any more than affliction and death can be purged from the tragedy of life itself.

*Oedipus* reminds me of the link between tragedy and ritual sacrifice. In one sense, as historian René Girard has argued, the threat of the undifferentiated chaos of plague demands a scapegoat be found and sacrificed. There are a lot of candidates in the play who could have been chosen for sacrifice. Oedipus is so determined. The sacrificial ritual is a call for obedience, law and order, a way of controlling the instincts and limiting freedom. In this sense, tragedy often seems to bring us back to a reasonable middle ground. It is the opposite of carnival and anarchy, Girard reminds us, but it can settle things down only for a short time. With

Shakespeare, we often have remnants of this kind of tragedy ("Something is rotten in the state of Denmark," for example), but I speculate that Shakespeare, despite his immersion in a late Renaissance culture with a growing respect for reason, is bursting with the energy of unreasonableness and with the knowledge that tragedy, like literature and language in general, always tends to overflow beyond the given boundary. And it is that overflow that is left over and helps create our desire to move forward.

*Shakespeare overflows the bounds of Aristotelean tragedy*

Then there is also what Keats said: Shakespeare is the great example of "negative capability." He loses himself in the character that he is creating. As a writer, Shakespeare is, to me, far removed from the Aristotelean version of Sophocles.

I say all this because you seem, at times, to argue that the Fool in *King Lear* helps us, as audience (or reader), to find the middle way; that Lear's belief that Cordelia might still live or that perhaps they both could become "God's spies," "taking on the mystery of things," is basically craziness, dementia run amuck. Many do read it that way. I read it differently.

To me, Shakespeare finds good ("It is very good," God says about all His creation) in each of his creations, in their uniqueness, in their craziness as well as their reasonableness. When Lear says to Cordelia that she has some cause to do him wrong, she enigmatically responds, "No cause, no cause." She is speaking then about unconditional love, but also about the nature of faith itself, the possibility that one could choose Jerusalem rather than Athens, faith rather than philosophical reason, and declaring that kind of choice as worthy and as human as any other choice. Lear may be foolish when he sees the feather stir with the breath of Cordelia on the other side of death, but I prefer to think that Shakespeare is not asking us simply to dismiss this demented fool of a man, but to ask ourselves whether there might be a difference between God's foolishness and man's. Perhaps Shakespeare is even thinking that, before tragic drama was invented, we had angels to help us receive messages.

Let me return, though, to the question of evolution (the crude becomes the sophisticated) vs. difference (there is no genuine progress, but uniqueness is always "good"). And let's assume a few propositions together for the moment:

That poetry precedes philosophy
That the beginning precedes the end
That darkness precedes light
That chaos precedes order
That the seed precedes the flower

I once asked a psychiatrist friend whether she thought shame was deeper than guilt. She replied that she didn't go for "deeper."

I then asked her, "How about, shame comes before guilt?" She was quick to agree.

She was thinking about science and a linear version of history, I assume. I was thinking about Freud and Jung, the unconscious, maybe even heaven and Earth.

I also said to her, "I believe in deep reading." She preferred the term *redescription* or *representation*. I was thinking about Coleridge and the imagination. She was thinking about cognitive science, the recent research on the brain. "We are both readers," I then suggested to her. "But where is the text we are supposedly reading?"

"Between us," she said. "It is a bit like the way the impressionists thought about color." How about Shelley? I wondered. And the "no place"—is that what she meant by "between us"? I wouldn't disagree with that.

The talking cure, the pharma cure— and the reading cure?

"In any case, we know the talking cure alone is not sufficient," she added. That she seemed to insist on. "The patient needs pharmaceutical medicine, the digestion of pills as much as he needs words and language, in order to calm disruption and boost serotonin levels. Celexa often helps." It's a brand name for citalopram, a medicine often prescribed to treat depression.

What about the book alive on the shelf, I wondered, and the need to write? But that was as far as we got that day. I thanked her for the conversation. "You're welcome," she replied. That was perhaps the most important moment in our conversation. Somehow, for that moment, she had granted me a gift of hope, call it a kiss if you will, an unconditional call to well-being and possibility without further demand or expectation. I am grateful to her.

As you know, David, I have lived for nine years now with Stage 4 neuro-endocrine pancreatic cancer. A miracle that I am grateful for as I continue on my way. At times, I take oxycodone to help relieve bouts of difficult pain. It is often a comfort, especially when I'm lying in bed at night, thinking in the darkness. My brilliant oncologist, who has saved my life several times now, believes, as I do, that oxycodone is an appropriate therapy for palliative care for terminal illness.

One day in his office, I mentioned to him that sometimes when I take oxycodone, my thinking seems to get better. There is a sudden clarity in the darkness, a sense that something blurry has suddenly come into the light. "Is this just an illusion?" I asked him.

He responded, as usual, with a somewhat enigmatic but always gentle smile: "Not 'better' but 'different,' " he said. I like that: *not better but different*. It opens the infinite possibilities of life, the unfinished business—including dialogue and ongoing interpretation. We were not speculating about progress or evolution that day, but the sense of difference, the potential that might not get one anywhere, but might offer a new perspective.

So let's change our assumptions for a moment:

> That philosophy is and is not poetry
> That the end is and is not at the beginning
> That eros and thanatos, living and dying, are and are not, are
>     both / and
> That we are always coming and going
> That light understands darkness, just as darkness understands
>     light, following each other wherever they wander

Language and silence make all this, and much more, possible. As the poet John Ashbery once put it, "Whenever I read a sentence, including a line of my own poetry, I am beset by the idea that it could have been written the other way." I think this is "good."

In a similar context, I might say that when I read and interpret, it is the sense of difference that I am attuned to.

When I think about poetry, or great novels, I think of them as a promise, a covenant made between writer and reader, a possibility that offers what is and what might be. What is and what is not. Literature keeps me human (I still use that old-fashioned word). It calls to me to carry on or go forth. It offers in its flow the possibility of "something else." It creates a difference—not so much a return home, but a potential for hope and protection from the idle chatter of the same, the established cultural pictures which, much like the Medusa's head, stop us cold, make us into hard stone.

In previous discussions, I have tried to mark out a difference between Hebrew and Greek in part because I imagine the difference as closely related to this belief I have about literature. I am not interested in the stone, but the event, the saying more than the said, the difference more than the same: for example, the dynamic movement of your poem "Chair" as it is created by the writer and recreated by the reader rather than the picture of the chair as an inanimate object pointed to at a distance.

Let me elaborate. The Israelites in the Hebrew Bible are basically materialists. This does not mean that they don't believe in God; they obviously do—a transcendent God who speaks with them on occasion, and once in a while walks with them on Earth. Nor does the notion that they are materialists intend to imply that they do not work for "good" or that they do not try to follow the Law (given on Mt. Sinai), or that they do not try to keep the promise of the covenant between God and themselves. But it does mean that they give little thought to heaven or hell (at least until the book of Daniel, late in the canon). To risk another generalization, Hebrew precedes Greek, privileges contingency over necessity, the particular over the universal, the experience over the abstraction, the dynamic event over the rock or the stone. The Ark, the so-called Tent of Meeting, is carried across the desert, in movement day after day. Only when the two temples are built (and too quickly destroyed) is such wandering movement temporarily halted.

For the Israelites then, at least at first, there is no Greek sense of self-evident truths, no foundation as such, no catechism or articles of faith, but an infinite skepticism (in the best sense of that term) as the rabbis with their endless and often contradictory interpretations of the Torah and Talmud later make clear. There is, in other words, always an alternative, found in each word, some would say each letter. Listen to the particular word, turn it and turn it, and then turn it again. The Jew, even in Israel, finds infinite possibilities in a grain of sand, in a blade of grass, in the particular, not the universal. We might even say that for the Jew, the unique, precious lives of Rosencrantz and Guildenstern are as important as the life of Hamlet himself. So, too, the Fool lost on the heath or the homeless wanderer out in the street.

To put it in other terms, the Jew lives in the midst of the messiness of this world and celebrates that living, even the suffering and pain of mortal life in its sentient being. This is the shout of *l'chaim*—admittedly not the howl of overwhelming affliction, but, yes, the celebration of life itself, with all its pain and suffering. We might even speculate that it is for similar reasons that changes in the moon make up the puzzling pattern of the Jewish calendar, in contrast to the one Platonic truth of the sun of the Greeks and the pagans. The Jews, in this regard, are the wanderers, the exiles, the other. (I would suggest that even in Israel, for many reasons, many not acceptable to me, they are far from feeling at home.)

The messy, painful life of the wanderer and the exile

As the poet Jabès puts it, "Do not ask the foreigner his place of birth, but the place he is going." At times, I think we are now all wanderers, migrants. Not *citizens* (a word which, for me, evokes the problem of privilege and a narcissistic sense of possession), but wanderers and temporary sojourners on this Earth that we do not own. Whether from the long corridor of slums surrounding Lagos or from Mexico or Syria, or from San Francisco or El Paso, Israel or Yemen, we are all on the move, listening for a counter story to disrupt the dominant lie of the mainstream culture, the one that takes various forms but appears on every screen that we stop to look at.

To put it again in slightly different terms, we are all in movement on the border of what is and what could be, intermingling eros and thanatos, life struggling with death. It is as if at times our organs and flesh are speaking out against their own destiny, a struggle of vowels against consonants, verbs against nouns, word against word, word within word (as the rabbis sometimes say)—and then of course the inevitability: the story is finished, mortal life has come to its end.

We are all born with a terminal illness. You can hear it in the cry of birth and the howl of death. How best then to live this one and only precious life we have been given? How best to make a difference under that sentence of terminal illness? That is the question that calls me on. I do not want to live someone else's life, but the one unique life granted to me. No one else but Bob Waxler can experience his death as he moves across the border, irreplaceable at that moment, alone—and no one else can replace the life of Bob Waxler, its detailed particulars, its unique messiness, its contradictions, its unpredictable joy and sorrow.

I have recently reread Tolstoy's *Death of Ivan Ilych*, partly because some current literary critics have suggested that Ilych has pancreatic cancer. Some details from the story might indicate this: his digestive problems, the sour tastes in his mouth, the location of his pain, the strange look in his eyes, the reluctance of doctors in the 19th century to inform patients about any terminal illness, the difficulty of diagnosing pancreatic cancer with minimal technology. But, of course, it is more than the question of Ilych's diagnosis that calls me now to Tolstoy. I find his death scenes fascinating—in part because Tolstoy wants to know what he cannot know, but yet insists on trying to know. To me, that is the mark of a serious writer. It is that insistence that demands the reader's attention and makes Tolstoy so troublesome and so magnificent. What is the meaning of pain? What is the meaning of death? Tolstoy wants to know.

In *Anna Karenina*, close to the middle of the book's long unfolding narrative, Levin and his young wife Kitty arrive at the deathbed of Levin's haunted brother Nikolai. Levin is anxious, disturbed, unable to comfort his brother (his bony body stripped down to its poverty), nor to find relief for himself. The small room emerges as a deteriorating environment of dirt and grime, smelling of death. Only Kitty seems to be able to move forward, to clean the room, to offer to Nikolai (raging with pain and affliction) moments of empathy and compassion. Through Kitty, Tolstoy manages to offer a temporary glimpse of what surely cannot last, but nevertheless hints at something else, another possibility, a difference.

Leaving the room after the inevitable death, though, Levin seems turned about by the event. Like literature itself, the event in its movement does not turn Levin to stone, but opens a new possibility for him (and the reader). Kitty announces that she is pregnant.

Tolstoy wants us to know that we often treat death simply as "the other," distancing ourselves from it, making it into an abstraction (like the syllogism, based on Kantian logic, that Ilych believes does not apply to him personally: "Caius is a man, men are mortal, therefore Caius is mortal"). We might briefly glimpse death in the vulnerable, almost naked eyes, of neighbors or strangers, brothers or sisters, all those who stand before us, but we still keep death at a convenient distance. But death is also within us, the unwritten which we, like Tolstoy, desire to know about, but cannot. Not the death of the other person, the death of Cassius, but the end of our own living breath, which is granted as a temporary gift to create our one and only story, that precious mortal life, singular and unique, which always ends alone.

As Ivan Ilych lies alone near the closing of his story, he begins a dialogue with death. He can no longer protect himself from it, no longer distance himself from it, no longer live the illusion of the lie, the abstraction that he, and most of the others, have been living. Alone in bed, in the midst of three days of pain and howling, he ponders the insoluble question that has in its wisdom finally opened to him: "What is this? Can it be death?" And then, as if responding to his painful call, he hears that other voice: "Yes, it is death."

The insoluble question: Can it be death?

Like Kitty in *Anna Karenina*, Gerasim, the Russian peasant in *The Death of Ivan Ilych*, is the only one who seems to have some sense of how to respond to the pain that death brings to life. Gerasim, close to the rhythm of the natural world, close to the rhythm of eros and thanatos, comforts Ilych now, not fearing to touch him, offering him empathy and compassion. It is an offer free of a sense of duty and possession, too; it seems unconditional, a gift with no expectation of return, simply an opening into the messiness of life and death itself.

As Ilych's pain intensifies and death draws closer, even his breath begins to betray him: "Suddenly some force struck him in the chest and side, making it still harder to breathe." And then Ilych "fell through a (black) hole, and there at the bottom was a light." For Ilych, like Levin in a different register, this, to me, also seems to suggest a turn in direction, another beginning, another possibility. Tolstoy—sounding here a little like a post-Einstein theoretical physicist—describes it this way: "like the sensation one sometimes experiences in a railway carriage when one thinks one is going backwards while one is really going forward and suddenly becomes aware of the real direction." Like Ilych, we, as readers, are also thrown forward.

Ilych might be destroyed by death, but, as Hemingway might say, he is not defeated by it. For Ilych, the abstract life—"the ratio of the square of the distance from death," as Tolstoy puts it—melts away, and the event of death ushers in the end of pain, offering in its place a somewhat mysterious sublime joy that arrives on the other side of fear and the illusion of hope. "Death is finished, he said to himself. It is no more! He drew in a breath, stopped in the midst of a sigh, stretched out and died."

This is Ivan Ilych. No one else. It is difficult to know what might occur beyond that moment when the breath leaves, stretches out like a body, and is then finished. But it is surely the uniqueness of this life that Tolstoy has given to us, what it was and what it was not under the sentence of death (terminal illness from the beginning). Unlike Ilych, though, after an interval, after stopping in the midst of a sigh, we, as readers, breathe again. We have reached a limit, and we carry on. Tolstoy has not given us an abstract truth here, but a singular creation of a particular mortal life. That is the genius of it. Ivan Ilych, for me, has become part of the immemorial past as well, a man who never actually existed, yet is always present now in the dream state of reading and thinking.

Tolstoy reminds me that what we cannot know is, at the deepest level, what we desire to know—or perhaps it is better to say what we long to know? That is what seems beyond the limits of what we, as finite beings, can grasp or give an absolute name to: what we often call God and death. To me, literature takes many different forms, serves us in many different ways, but it is particularly important when it moves towards these two mysteries. That is, when it takes a stand at the border between us as human beings and that which we long for (God / death). It is as if through literature we can, on occasion, open a dialogue with the silence which we cannot properly name, which we cannot properly know or grasp.

Walter Benjamin makes a crucial point in this context when he discusses, in his brilliant essay "The Storyteller," how the ancient writers used to find their inspiration as a kind of call through God, while now modern writers are compelled to write as if in response to a call from death. (Of course, David, you and I have also raised this idea in our previous exchanges.) Sometimes, I believe (or at least long to believe) that if we listen closely, we can still hear that voice of God; we can be inspired by it. Other times, death itself whispers out of its silence, reminding us of the need to respond somehow to that silence, to what often appears, not as a kind of fullness of meaning (as God might indicate) but as the ultimate lack of meaning or purpose.

There was a time when prophets and literary writers acquired inspiration from God, or from the Muses, or from dictation offered by angels, or from the call of that no place (which we have discussed off and on). Leaning forward, the writer might hear the voice roaring like thunder or a still small voice like a whisper in the breath of the world. Or he might, like you, David, hear music coming from some other place. By contrast, in modern times, it is more often death that calls the writer to respond, but that, too, is a call that seems often to come from no place, from a silence that compels the writer to listen and respond, to continue to move forward, yet also long to discover what cannot be known.

The writer, in either situation, must dare to create. He moves to the edge of human consciousness, the boundary between this mortal world and the no place that cannot be grasped. He is also aware, one imagines, that when he moves to the edge to listen, he intensifies all risk. Like Freud, he senses that pain and death cannot be assimilated into what mortal humans often call "civilized man." The writer must acknowledge that he is one of "the discontents."

What can he do, though? He has arrived at the liminal point. If he is Shakespeare, he might at times write tragedy, deferring, postponing, delaying as long as possible the inevitable end. If he is Conrad, he might offer a choice between Kurtz (a man who crosses over the border, enters fully into the horror of the heart of darkness) and Marlow (a man who steps back from the horror yet must continue on with his own pain and suffering—and his own set of lies).

The writer cannot be satisfied as "the civilized man"; he is inevitably a discontent. He works with that "chaos again" (as you point out), the leftovers, the remainder, the shadows and the unseen, the overflow and the unwritten. _Being civilized is not enough_

But what does "chaos" mean? According to the poet and translator Willis Barnstone, the Greek word _khaos_ originally translates as "gaping"—a groundless void, a yawning. At the very beginning, the Hebrew Bible seems to suggest a "nothingness," later associated by some commentators with the trackless vacancy of the desert. In "The Marriage of Heaven and Hell," Blake claims that when an angel looked into this kind of chaos, he saw only monsters, but for Blake, out of the chaos emerges a vision of a harpist singing. Nietzsche, sounding a little like Blake here, claims you must immerse yourself in chaos if you want to give birth to a dancing star. (Perhaps this also touches on your vision, David, of "dark order" as you see it in *King Lear*?)

To me, chaos is the messiness of life itself, the confusion and entanglements, the paradoxes and the contradictions, the pain and pleasure, joy and sorrow that make up the flow of the events of living and dying. The writer ties and unties these knots, helps us to see why it is worth going forth. And the reader too makes the journey through language, out toward the border. Each attempt is a new attempt, just as each reading of a book is a new reading, not seeking abstraction or self-evident truth, but entering into the motion of the experience, the bodying forth of the messiness of our own unique mortal existence and the endless interpretation of it.

It is this kind of thinking that often sends me back to the Hebrew Bible now, a topic that I want to continue to explore as we expand further our discussions. I will save some of that for next time, though. Before I finish here, however, let me reiterate my belief that literature is the best way we have today to enchant the mortal world. That enchantment comes through the gift of language, perhaps inspired by God, perhaps driven by the silence of death as that silence moves through our finite senses. I admit that sometimes I like to believe what Coleridge (through the German Romantics) believed: that the imagination can reenact a repetition of the infinite I Am, and so it can create enchanted poetry, similar, but not the same, as the work of the original Creator Himself.

More reasonably, perhaps, I embrace the supreme fiction that Wallace Stevens talks about, the sense that language coupled with imagination on our finite human scale is a "a fiction," but the kind of fiction that creates for us the beauty and glory of mortal existence. This kind of creation through language is a fortunate one for us. It is, though, not the self-evident truth of the Greek philosophers, nor the logos of the Gospel according to John or the church fathers who follow. Nor is it connected to the cause / effect reason of rational science or the perfect reason of Kant and his followers. Nor is it a belief that we can find in signs pointing outward (and certainly not through allegory) an essence that leads to closure, to the abstracted truth, to the closing of a perfect circle, to the end of anything.

For me, it is the language of literature, always opening a space for the reader, calling the reader to respond, that keeps us alive, that makes the difference.

Bob

# 30. Better Not to Be Born?

Bob,

I'm taken with your ruminations on the issue of birth and death, particularly the notion that we are born with our own death in place as terminal illness. Taking that further, some Greek (and before that, Buddhist) thinking around anti-natalism, formalized by Hegesias of Cyrene as "philosophical pessimism," holds that it would be better not to be born; that life's pain is inevitably stronger than its pleasure or happiness. This idea is reinforced in Genesis by God when, after the fall, he banishes Adam and Eve from Eden to lives of hardship. I could imagine that they then might have wished they had never been born. And in Ecclesiastes, the preacher asks, what good is it to work and suffer? Isn't the subtext that the best fate would be not to have been born?

The brute fact, for which no religion has had an answer, is that none of us ask to be born.

In tough times, this is a seductive, even comforting idea, though quite alien to most thinking this side of antiquity, and especially on our shores: American optimism has no serious place for this depth of pessimism.

Is that because we haven't, as a culture, suffered enough for it to trickle down to the citizen on the street? We have enslaved and denigrated people, forced them to live in misery—but has anti-natalism caught on, even with them?

Enter, as refutation, the Judeo-Christian belief in an afterlife. The reward for suffering will get paid in heaven! Look beyond this veil of tears to our just deserts in Elysian Fields. Though "just" here is a little scary.

After death, is "justice" really want we want?

Where am I on this? I'm in flux, with no fixed immutable rock on which to stand. And the existentialists? Sartre seems to say that an afterlife exists if you choose it to. But how is that more than intellectual pablum? Somewhere in this position is condescension, though I can't quite smoke it out.

I daresay many have moved away from religion in order to escape, on the one hand, the weight of pessimism, and on the other, the necessity of accepting the unprovable doctrine of redemption in an afterlife. As for me, I like the humanist movement in this context.

Are light and darkness proper metaphors for moving this discussion forward? They are, unfortunately, absolutes, which is too bad, as they both have shades upon shades within them. I think you were grappling with this when, in your last, you wrote "that light understands darkness, just as darkness understands light."

For me, this approach evokes the role of the playwrights, who possess the ability to understand all the characters they write, all the colors in their palette. And so, as the playwright, Shakespeare must understand Edgar and Edmund, Goneril and Cordelia., Lear and the Fool. And not just superficially, but down to their souls. Failing to do so will result in an inferior play, one weighted toward a moral viewpoint rather than embracing what a tragedy aims for: awe and pity in the face of not this character or that, but the human condition. Or what comedy strives for: relief from the terror of mortality

How about the poet in this regard? Let's consider some examples.

Milton? I am not a close reader of *Paradise Lost,* but as I recall Milton does not understand Satan so much as condemn him.

Dante? He understands his main character (ironically, himself), and his guide, Virgil, but does he extend the same understanding to the many sinners suffering in Hell? No. All he presents, and all we know, is that they defied God; they sinned and are being punished. Dante's is truly a medieval grasp of behavior. Remove God's commandments from the poem, and it makes no sense, unless we deem Dante, the writer, a sadist.

The psychiatrist friend you quote disappoints me in this regard, although I am quite taken with how your conversation ended—with her simple comment, "you're welcome," expressing something deep and giving you hope.

The life-changing power of deep reading

Yet, earlier, she eschews the talking cure. What about the *reading* cure? You and I both have a deep faith, based on lived experience, in the curative and life-changing power of deep reading. Does she? And if not, why not?

I also love deep talking. I have lived experience in this, too, and know its power. I talked out my life over many years with a therapist with a gift for listening and responding, often with questions, occasionally with wisdom, and always with my good in mind. The result for me was a nearly immeasurable deepening of understanding, and living proof of the adage, "Feel deeply, and change will come of its own accord."

I now ask whether your multiyear experience with cancer has had similar benefits. Has it been a pathway to deeper understanding of yourself and your life—understanding you might not have attained otherwise? I suspect so and hope so.

And what about your brilliant oncologist, for whom I have a very good feeling—he who knows the difference between better and different. Is his wisdom now your own?

This is perhaps over against your remarkable poem:

> The doctor just walked in
> White coat soaked in gin
> And stethoscope in red
> With small metal head
> Cold to the touch,
> And its dangling rubber feet
> Like a puppet you might meet;
> It's like high-tech
> Hanging from his neck.
> And check those blue suede
> shoes and hound dog pants
> A traveling nurse
> Up from Memphis rants,

Shake, rattle, roll
Elvis lives in Idaho,
It's all spectacle these days
An image on a screen
Usually blurry, often mean.

I respond to the poem's tone, and what isn't said, as strongly as to what is said. What isn't said is what situation is being described. Is the speaker a patient? Why does the patient require a doctor? And what kind of doctor is this, with a "white coat soaked in gin?" A faker or a quack? As the poem unwinds (or, like a clock, winds up) it becomes increasingly surreal, which is a strength. If the speaker were a character in a play, one would think he's hallucinating, or disturbed. All fascinating.

Then there's the meter and rhyme. Set in iambic tetrameter, the poem is in good company. Shakespeare, of course, where the 4-beat line often stands in contrast to the 5-beat, often for emphasis and mood change. Byron and Wordsworth also come to mind as practitioners. But I've never seen a rhyme scheme like this (AABB CDDE FGHH IJJ), and I suspect it was unplanned, meaning that rhymes came to you spontaneously, with no strain, and went away equally easily. This gives the poem a genuineness that is charming, engaging, authentic.

As for tone, I'd describe it as mock-sarcastic, and very appropriate if I posit that the speaker, as patient, is in possibly desperate straits and therefore taking solace in rejecting the seriousness of his plight. Mock epic comes to mind as a model (aided by all line beginnings being in upper case, a throwback for modern poetry).

The last couplet is particularly memorable, with the image on a screen being "Usually blurry, often mean." This, preceded by my favorite line, capping off Elvis's brief appearance: "It's all spectacle these days."

What is all spectacle? Medicine? Life? The reader is left not knowing, but sure that the speaker knows the answer.

Then, "Double Helix," a poem in an altogether different vein:

In the beginning is the end
And
In the end is the beginning;

I look back to see the future
And
Forward to the past;

The horizon unfolds
Before me
And
After me;

Ahead
And
Behind,

Ascending
And
Descending,

Like a bluebird
Between
Two angels
From
Paradise.

Here, in the first person, your rumination on DNA and its function, both for an individual and (I think) for a culture.

The first two stanzas are close enough to the opening of Eliot's "Burnt Norton" to beg comparison:

Time present and time past
Are both perhaps present in time future,
And time future contained in time past.

In fact, the poem seems reluctant to move past the aura of Eliot and the comparison, until the remarkable simile of the last five lines. It takes us far afield from any source or comparison, to a mysterious place with a bluebird between two angels. Here I feel that we are in very personal terrain, your innermost awareness of and, perhaps, *need* for the horizon to unfold "Like a bluebird / Between / Two angels / From paradise." With a poet's daring, and prerogative, the poem's vision is of an unexpected calm and spiritually nurturing place leagues from the double helix, and science itself, where the horizon unfolds. The essence of this place? In Russian and other mythologies, the bluebird stands for hope. If the hope of the discoverers of the double helix was that we would finally understand the structure of life, the poem's hope is of another magnitude—that whatever our genetic makeup, as living souls we yearn always for enlightenment and wisdom, something brought by the two angels from paradise. And something in no way addressed by science.

Sidenote: Lear invokes the inanimate with "O you are men of stone." To not see Cordelia's (and his) suffering is to not be human. Despair is the opposite of hope, and for Lear to witness hope's demise by not weeping in the moment when Cordelia's breath fails would be to trade away his humanity, equivalent, in our discussion, to cashing in the promise of the double helix for silence and death. In the parlor game of bringing historical figures together for conversation, I'd pay full admission to hear Shakespeare, Watson, and Crick have a go over beer and sandwiches.

I am struck that when God calls his creation good, he is fully indulging in radical understatement, even with the modifier "very." Presuming that God of the Old Testament knew, and of course could see, everything about his universe, he knew what, thanks to the James Webb telescope, we know now. And what we are now seeing is outrageously spectacular. So shouldn't God have pronounced his creation something more than "good"? Couldn't he at least have pronounced it spectacular? Of course, this begs the question of what the Old Testament God actually knew. Did he know anything, or is He Himself the creation of writers of the time, and so actually could know no more than they did? Just as Lear could know no more than Shakespeare did.

I resonate strongly with your thoughts on all of us being wanderers and migrants, vs. citizens or, I might add, inhabitants.

At the same time, I understand the strong pull many feel in the opposite direction. That being a citizen or inhabitant is actually a hard-won and much-needed reprieve from the fear of wandering.

This is a fear that I suppose I cannot know; but have I actually been tested? I have never been a refugee, or even an immigrant.

I find it interesting that a much-used current word for death is "passing." Very much in vogue. "Mr. Jones passed yesterday." Passed to where? I hear it not only from people in full acceptance of an afterlife, for whom the passing would make sense. I hear it from all manner of non-believers.

Now, the term "passed away" would bring some sense to bear, in that the "away" part is not followed with a specific locale.

I can leave the room, and you have a clear picture of that action even though I give no hint as to where I plan (or hope) to arrive upon leaving. That is what "passing away" evokes. But without the preposition "away," the image is much less clear.

All that aside, of course I also resonate strongly with "No one else but Bob Waxler can experience his death . . . alone. No one else can replace the life of Bob Waxler."

This is a courageous and moving assertion, my friend. And a true anchor to hold onto.

I hope next time to take you up on meditations on Tolstoy.

David

# 31. Cleaving to the Edge of Hope

David,

T hanks so much for your response to my two poems. Your comments send me back to *Echo Aonides* and our collaboration in those sparkling and confusing times under the banner of St. Augustine: "When the Muses fail, so does man's spirit, and so, alas, does civilization also."

"Double Helix" (so abstract that only "the blue bird" can light the way) and "The Guitar Man" (an attempt to disrupt the abstract and the screen culture with a gyroscopic rhythm), are both recent poems written some sixty-odd years after our *Echo Aonides*. (I do want to make it clear, by the way, that my extraordinary oncologist might be the bluebird but certainly not the guitar man.)

Literature meant everything to us in those old halcyon days. The English Romantics provided the poetry and the vision, Dylan the songs, and, yes, even Eliot and Pound excited our dreams of something new, something evermore about to be.

We were young, and we believed that the best way to judge a society and a culture was to measure how inclusive it was, how open it was, how passionate and energetic it could be. It was the 1960s and literature, we were convinced, could lead us beyond the horizon.

More than a half century has passed since those expansive days, but, like you sitting beside a pool not so many months ago, I too still hear music as I go. I like to believe that some of that music flows through those two recent poems I sent you as well—music connected to the mystery of voice and to the hand that writes; music that provides a glimpse of ongoing possibility; music that I hear as well in your response to those two recent inventions of mine, a response that sends me across sixty years of time, as I sit here now in the present moment, a gift from you, an opening which I am grateful for.

I still believe that literature can change lives, that literature is our best hope for democracy, that reading and writing can keep us alive, that language prevents the world from collapse.

At times, reading and writing for me now in 2024 has become somewhat like prayer. As the French philosopher Anne Dufourmantelle defines it, "Prayer is a state of waiting for a word that you know will not come, but at the same time, is there inside you, deposited there from time immemorial."

Dufourmantelle reminds me that I was born from another, thrown into the language of others, carried and nourished by others, but I will die alone. Between these two remarkable and apparently incompatible events, as she says, an "impossible dialogue takes place." In *The Risk of Reading*, I explored this notion in a different context, attempting to uncover the tension between our connectivity to others and our uniqueness. In terms of creating narrative fiction and deep reading, I put it this way:

> Like an adventurous journey, both narrative telling and deep reading are always questing, stirring desire and reflection, revealing and concealing, moving us backwards and forward, in an attempt to deepen our understanding of both our uniqueness and connectivity as human beings.

I want to know what we cannot know: the word that will not come, but that I sense has always been there from the beginning. How else could Dufourmantelle have put this impossible possibility, this excruciating tug of language to outdo itself? I would agree that it is a kind of prayer. Through language more slanted than Emily Dickinson's, Dufourmantelle (the philosopher turned poet) hints at what I believe reading and writing can offer us: "the absolute opening to the unhoped for."

Reading makes the impossible dialogue possible

186

Through my discussions with you, through my reading and writing, through my experiences with others, I follow traces that resonate with me as I seek that "absolute opening to the unhoped for." It is not an abstract conceptual truth unmoored from the flow of my experience that I am seeking, but an ongoing turning toward the other. It is always a dialogue, a call demanding a response. It is as if I am always listening or speaking, walking along the way.

I hear the voice of Whitman bumming on the American road, Baudelaire as flâneur walking with the rhythm of spleen in the new city streets, Jabès moving to the sound of shifting sands in the vast desert.

There is in all those voices a longing Wordsworth well knew, for "something evermore about to be." To me, this is what Dufourmantelle means when she uses the phrase "the absolute opening to the unhoped for." It is what I hear each time I read your little poem "Chair," as it rocks back and forth, invites me as a reader to join it, and then surprises me as it throws me forward. It is the voice, the saying of the chair, not its said but its saying, that makes the difference for me. It is the poem as it opens in the flow of our common language and creates through the voice not the chair as thing but the chair as movement—this is what sings for me. Rilke put it this way:

> I so love to hear the singing of things
> You touch them—and they fall as silent as stone . . .

It is not the stone I seek, but the word in movement, the word always saying and unsaying itself, revealing and concealing that which I cannot finally or absolutely know, but which I do know has been there from the beginning. To pursue that mystery is worth the risk. It is the risk of reading.

I have chosen a life of reading and writing, and am thankful for it, just as I am thankful for our friendship and for the blazing shooting stars in the night sky and the blue flame on the Sabbath candles silently burning down just before a new week begins. "I so love to hear the singing of things." There is something unique in the voice just as there is something unique in the walk of each individual. Long before I can see the face of a friend coming toward me, I can often identify him by his walk, by his unique style. So, too, with the voice. It is the voice of my father (or of my mother) that I often sense in remembrance (*zakhor*). I mention this now because I am thinking about the way voice is connected to walking, somewhat like the connection between speaking and writing, or the connection between listening and reading. Whitman and Baudelaire knew that. Thoreau certainly knew it. In his essay on "Walking," for example, he makes clear his belief that there is a wildness about walking that starts in the feet and spreads through the body, enhancing circulation through the heart, and expanding thinking as it excites the imagination and the brain.

The movement of the body and the flow of words in literature

Again, it is the flow of the voice—the movement of the body walking, the singing of things that has its own mystery—yes, that flow of words which distinguishes language and literature from most other activities in my life.

Maurice Blanchot insisted that the Hebrew Bible was what he called "The Law of the Walking Feet." Since the time of Abraham, the covenant between God and man was always in movement just as the Jewish people were. The engagement with the polysemous language of the Bible and the dialogical sense of relationship that such engagement implies was, for Blanchot, I imagine, somewhat like the exercise of walking: from the movement of the walking feet, the circulation of blood to the heart (the place of both feeling and thinking in Hebrew tradition) can bring joy and understanding. Ideas do not become clots of blood threatening life, but rather flow to the heart creating a life of compassion and a glimpse of understanding.

According to Jewish tradition, God gave Moses at Mt. Sinai both the oral Torah and the written Torah simultaneously. The Hebrew Bible (and the Talmud) then can be thought of as open to infinite interpretations but no final and complete understanding. In post-modern terms, we might say the Bible offers "the absolute opening to the unhoped for." Human understanding then becomes contextual and unique to each listener (or reader), but yet that listener (or reader) is always in dialogue with others.

This is a way of reading that has increasingly helped me to appreciate more fully the wonder and mystery of the impossible meeting between our uniqueness and our connection to others, between death and life, between silence and voice. Such thinking

188

has allowed me new insights into my reading of Tolstoy, for example (as I have suggested in earlier discussions with you) and also my reading of Kafka, who in his story "Beyond the Law" suggests that there is a unique door granted to each of us, if we dare to walk across its threshold. It is a kind of reading that calls me to the voice of the language and to my relationship with the language as I listen, and it is the kind of reading that reminds me each time I re-read a poem or a novel, that the text has not changed, but I have. And that, too, makes all the difference. It is in the depths of the language that all this happens.

In *The Risk of Reading*, following others, I considered this exploration of the depths of language "deep reading," and commented on it:

> Deep reading is a risky and rewarding encounter with our rhythms and needs, our own feeling and emotions, and it offers a way of making sense with that encounter. Through such reading, we discover how we are all connected to others and to our own evolving stories. We experience our own plots and stories unfolding through the imaginative language and voice of others, and we desire to move on.

I agree with what I wrote then (in 2014), but it is far from complete in its thinking or its implications. It seems to emphasize our connections to others, the way we make sense of our encounters with the world, the reward of the encounter with the rhythm and needs of our own self. I don't disagree with any of that. But I also see other stories emerging from that one back in 2014. Out from the notion of the embrace and connections with others (a relationship crucial to a life of flourishing) also emerges the importance of the notion of uniqueness, what might also be called the aloneness of that life (that one and only precious life that each of us is given). And, yes, there is perhaps a further addition to this difficult paradox: call it the unique and invisible voice deposited in the midst of it all from the beginning.

When I first read *The Catcher in the Rye* in 1960 and discussed it with my high school friends, we all agreed that Holden Caulfield was a rebel who didn't want to hang around with the phonies of this world, disliked celebrities, avoided idle chatter. Our English teacher told us that the novel typified the inevitable transition we all must make from innocence to experience, from childhood to adulthood. Eventually, we, too, would become adults. My friends and I concluded that our teacher was the phony. Holden was a rebel and a friend.

Sixty years later, I still like Holden, but, for me, the novel now offers an entirely different reading experience. When I listen to his unique and wounded voice as it emerges from the language of the novel, I sense his vulnerability, his desperate desire for dialogue, his egotism and his generosity. It is as if I am obligated to pay attention to him, to acknowledge his call. If I close the book, Holden will die.

When I think about Holden's story today, I think about Salinger's own experience in World War II, about the flow of dialogue, about the importance of voice in the telling of a story, and I also think about some of our own discussions about the Holocaust, about the nature of silence, and about my own personal pain from cancer. All that becomes an inevitable part of my context now when reading Salinger, when walking through his language.

Isn't Salinger struggling with his own traumatic experience? As a Jew and as a writer, perhaps he is thinking not only about his own time in World War II, but about the Holocaust. I wonder. Certainly he is attempting to find a way to engage with the mid-century disruption and trauma of disappearance. And isn't Holden primarily struggling with a similar problem? The silence and disappearance of a brother he cared about, the undreamt impossibility having become possible, the death of human kinship.

July 18, 1946: That is the death of his brother, a date which otherwise would be long forgotten, I imagine. But it is not by mere chance that it is the only date mentioned in Holden's narrative. I am willing to bet that most readers have forgotten it (if they ever noticed it). But it is the only date that Holden can remember. It is as if that date of disappearance has become the immemorial past for Holden, the word that you are waiting for that you know will never come, but at the same time, it is there inside you, deposited there from now and forever. It is not a rock or a stone to build on, a foundation for future celebration, but rather a no place, a cry or a scream calling to Holden, just as Holden calls to us. It sanctions his story, though, and authorizes his ethical demand for the response of the reader.

Where do the ducks in Central Park go in the wintertime? This is the question that obsesses Holden. He'd like to know the answer. It haunts him like it would anyone after such terror. And every time he crosses a road, he tells us, he feels like he is disappearing. His very existence is at stake. "It was that kind of crazy afternoon, terrifically cold, and no sun out or anything, and you felt like you were disappearing every time you crossed the street." Holden is addressing us directly, that "you" which is each one of us; he needs us to feel it, that cold terror, that sunless day, that disappearance.

Is this also then a version of that no place which we have been talking about in our discussions, a silent voice that can disrupt ordinary human existence, an unspeakable event that yet must be spoken about? It cannot be spoken about directly, but, as Dickinson said, it must be spoken indirectly—that is, at a slant. Salinger understood this, I am sure. It could not be explained, but it could not be forgotten either. Maybe this was what Salinger was hinting at when he said that it was not Rupert Brooke but Emily Dickinson who was the best war poet.

Speaking about the unspeakable

Holden struggles to create his life again, to create something out of the nothing that surrounds him. That nothingness is not emptiness, though, but life as he knows it in the moment. He cannot answer the question that he asks (Where do the ducks go?), but he does not give up asking. Eventually he does acknowledge that it is impossible to erase the graffiti on the walls of buildings (including the school that his sister Phoebe attends), nor can he erase the marks on the gravestones visible in the cemetery. Nor can he protect the innocent before they fall over the edge of the rye field. Nor can he save his sister from falling off the merry-go-round.

As readers, we might ask, what can Holden do? What can be done for Holden? We can listen, Salinger seems to say. Listen to Holden's unique voice telling the story from a rest home just on the other side of trauma. It is a voice haunted by the invisible, by the no place that flows through him, by the date that cannot be grasped, by the meeting with a brother who will always, now and forever, be missed. We can listen closely to that voice.

Salinger insisted that *The Catcher in the Rye* never be made into a film. Holden's unique voice should not, and could not, be made visible. As Holden says at the beginning of his narrative, he is not going to tell us another typical Dickens-like story—the type of story with a beginning, then a middle, then an end. His telling will be counter to type. I take this as a call from Holden for the reader to pay attention.

As Rilke said, seek out the singing, not the stone. Holden will not build from hard rock, from a stable and culturally acceptable foundation, from preconceived notions of cause and effect. Rather, he will disrupt and plead with us, call for a response from us. Holden's life depends on it.

My old high school teacher was not wrong when he suggested that *The Catcher in the Rye* was about the transition from childhood to adulthood. Holden might even have had a temporary case of arrested development. After a short rest, he'd probably get over some of what he suffers. My teacher was not completely right, though. For me today, the language of the novel resonates within a different context. I hear different discussions from my own life and the life of others rising up from the language in the novel. I glimpse the contradictions of finite life through that language and the possibility of human agency through dialogue within those contradictions. But I also sense that, at least for Salinger, Holden's unique voice is as close as the writer can come to the unique life, the one and only precious and vulnerable life of Holden himself. It is the life of each reader, too: the one and only life now and forever haunted by the mystery of disappearance, a sense of leaving without return.

Our one and only life, precious and haunted

There is no return here, no ultimate conversion, but a never-ending going forth (including a turning toward the other), a shout from the writer to the reader, a call from Holden for my response. It is a way of keeping each other alive: a testament to reading and writing, and a courageous attempt at the edge of the world to give voice to an opening that might yet lead to the unhoped for.

Such musing about the matter of voice evokes another time and another place. In 1974, I started teaching at Whitman College in Walla Walla, Washington. It was a one-year contract in the wild West, and by the end of the year, my wife Linda, our two young boys, and I were all happy enough to be headed back to New England.

There were some wonderful times at Whitman, though. One in particular stands out at the moment—the day I hosted Ken Kesey when he came to the campus. At my house, he told me a little-known story about his attempt to write a screenplay for his novel *One Flew Over the Cuckoo's Nest.* I see now that it is connected to our discussion about the power of voice.

Kesey had been asked to write the screenplay, but when he submitted it to the producers it was rejected almost immediately. They paid him a small sum for his effort and then hired another writer for the film (which, as we all know, became a box-office smash). The producers told Kesey that his version would never work with a popular audience.

Why not? What had Kesey done? As he explained it to me one afternoon in Walla Walla, he had attempted to do what he had done in his novel. His screenplay kept Chief Bromden, "the half-breed" Native American (the invisible American), central to the film. In the novel, the chief's unique voice tells the story. It is his language that creates our experience as readers. It is as if the world passes through his consciousness, embodied in his language. As the chief says about his story, it is true even if it didn't happen.

According to Kesey, the film that won a dozen Academy Awards had little relation to his novel. He seemed still upset about the whole business.

I doubt Kesey ever thought about his link to Salinger, but my point here is that, like Salinger, Kesey (I imagine) had in his novel created a unique voice through the flow of language, a voice that offered to the reader the experience of the contradictions and complexities of a unique life, a life which included a sense of disappearance, even vanishing. That the flow of visible images on a screen could be substituted for the flow of the language of the book might indicate part of the problem Kesey ran into. It is the kind of problem that would become increasingly clear over the next fifty years as the screen culture, with its emphasis on images rather than words, surface rather than depth, began to dominate, if not destroy, the traditional book culture. That the chief (the invisible American) deserved to be heard, in any case, was clearly also part of the issue for Kesey. It was his voice that was central in the novel, but the producers had other ideas in mind for the film.

When the screen culture is inadequate

The blockbuster film marginalized the chief, offered instead a preconceived and culturally acceptable abstraction: McMurphy vs. Big Nurse, rebellion vs. repression. The chief's voice was lost in the allegory, in the iconic and powerful images seen through the technology of a screen culture. The singing threatened to become a stone.

It is not surprising that at the end of Kesey's novel, the chief is on the road, headed out beyond the boundaries of the United States. In the film, the chief, despite his significant size, is pushed far into the margins, barely visible at all.

I remember now another time, another moment concerning the voice. 1982: enjoying an NEH (National Endowment for the Humanities) summer fellowship at Princeton, I am at a party when Joyce Carol Oates arrives. She has spent the afternoon with Norman Mailer in Manhattan and is filled with interesting stories about the encounter. No doubt she admires Mailer's rebellious spirit and literary talent, but she cannot dismiss his inexcusable treatment of women.

Today, her most interesting remarks emerge when she mentions Mailer's comments about voice. Oates says that Mailer insisted that he could not find his authentic voice. It was not that he felt that he had lost his voice, but that he was no better than an amateur ventriloquist. This was especially true, Mailer apparently said, when he wrote novels. To Oates, this was all foolishness.

I am not sure where Mailer got this idea, especially the connection of his own voice to ventriloquism. I have always thought that Mailer was basically part of the Romantic tradition, though, and he might have gotten such an idea from the English Romantics, especially from Coleridge, who was fascinated by the development of the art of ventriloquism at the beginning of the 19th century. For Coleridge, the ventriloquist, like the poet, was always challenged by questions related to voice. Was the authentic voice transcendental or immanent? How does the voice move from the poet to the poem? From the ventriloquist to the rag doll? Do we admire the natural sense of the voice or the artistic talent of the speaker? To what extent is the audience required to suspend disbelief? And so on.

What is the source of this elusive thing we call "authenticity"?

I remember agreeing with Oates when she claimed that Mailer was being foolish about all this business concerning ventriloquism. "Whose voice wrote all those novels? Wasn't that Mailer?" I joked with her at the time. But when I consider it now, I can better understand Mailer's point. Rereading his novels, I sense they are not his best work. There is something false in those voices, something put on. I find his best work in his "new journalism," a genre that he helped to create. There is an authenticity in *The Executioner's Song*, for example, a work that he had recently written when Oates went to see him. Perhaps that's what he was talking about that day.

I will never know for sure. But that discussion with Oates in 1982 about the voice of the writer also shapes the way I read now. It also helps provide the context of the way I encounter the world, the way I meet it, coming and going. It emerges as I write to you, David my friend, and as I listen for the singing of things, anticipating dialogue wherever I go.

The Voice. I want to know what I cannot know about it. Is it somehow connected to the roaring voice that Moses heard on Mt. Sinai? Is it the fiery voice of YHWH inscribing for all of us the ten words on stone tablets? Or is it connected to the still small voice that Elijah also heard at Mt Sinai much later in time, if not in myth?

I want to know.

Bob

# 32. "Won't Writing Commercially Kill Your Poetry?"

Bob,

I 've been happily drawn into your exploration of essential realities.

Your question: "How best then to live this one and only precious life we have been given?"

Your rumination: "Tolstoy reminds me that what we cannot know is, at the deepest level, what we desire to know."

And your final declaration: "I want to know."

As a creed, this last takes stamina and courage. With those earlier queries of yours, it drives me to Blake (maybe I wanted to go to him anyway). I am pleased with this, partly because Blake has not loomed large for me for some time, and partly because I closely associate him with you—your deep reading of him and your lifelong teaching.

As preliminary, I turn to your high school English teacher who, in reference to *The Catcher in the Rye*, saw Holden Caulfield in transition from innocence to experience, childhood to adulthood—a notion that you and your friends roundly rejected in favor of a more pure take on Holden—that of rebel. (Ah, the clarity of young conviction!) I shared this view of course, and saw also a *soupçon* of existential sorrow in his psyche: the unconscious sorrow of being a rebel—someone apart. Or was this my own similar early sorrow, for me a vague bass note backing up a stronger happiness, even joy, deriving from my choice to defy upbringing and circumstances and to choose literature and poetry for my life? If so, I'm sure I projected my turmoil onto Salinger's fictional character.

By your own admission, your view of Holden has changed radically as you have grown through experience. And mine? I venture that my existential sorrow functioned as a kind of spotlight that, whenever I looked toward Holden, snapped on, to reveal him as he was but also as I wanted him to be.

Back to Blake. Spending time, after long separation, with *Songs of Innocence and Experience,* confirms that it's a good choice right now. If we accept that life is, as your teacher would have it, movement from innocence to experience, then Blake is our poet.

First, definitions. What is innocence? Legally, I'm innocent if I'm shown not to have committed some crime in question. This is clearly not Blake's version of the concept. Spiritually, the Bible's concept of innocence revolves around absence of sin and iniquity. We can add lack of guile or corruption, certainly. Do these ancient definitions cover modern life now, post-Freud, post-modernism? I'm not sure. But they seem close to Blake's usage.

For pre-moderns, when Adam and Eve ate the fruit (a metaphor for all but literalists, even in the iron age?), the couple traded innocence for worldly knowledge, "knowledge of good and evil." So, by that idea, if I search for knowledge and / or mine what depths I can to understand good and evil, or much else in the ethical realm, do I lose my innocence?

By saying, "I want to know," am I facilitating just such loss of innocence? Was Blake?

This seems biased toward ignorance being a better place to be than knowledge. Then why do we strive for knowledge? To actually rid ourselves of innocence? Where might Blake be in this? What did he think and what did he know?

Does innocence equal ignorance?

In the first poem in *Song of Innocence*, which Blake calls "Introduction," Blake inserts himself, in first person, as the one "piping songs of pleasant glee." The result? He sees a child on a cloud who, on hearing the piping, first laughs, then weeps ("he wept with joy to hear"). When the boy vanishes, Blake plucks a reed to make, not a flute, but a pen:

And I wrote my happy songs
Every child may joy to hear.

In spite of dealing with Blake's writing here, my intent is otherwise—I want ultimately to not dwell on what Blake wrote, but rather to ask, "What did Blake know?"

As *Songs of Innocence* unfolds all the way to "The Little Boy Lost" and "The Little Boy Found," I, as reader, feel as if I've been ushered into a garden of (mostly) delights, exposed to a small family of father, mother, child, where very little can seriously go wrong. Then, embarking on the subsequent *Songs of Experience*, the opposite takes hold, with the likes of the tiger and lost children populating a more dire world.

But again, it's not Blake's words, songs, poems, or music I want to penetrate. It's his mind. What did Blake know that fed his poetry? My sense is that his knowledge, of life and himself, is paramount, holding sway over his life and writing in a unique way less obvious in other poets, Romantic or not.

What was his special insight? I think that he knew profoundly the dilemma of being a child in an adult world. And of being a sensitive, aware adult in a world run by other adults, many of whom seek power, and not just the power that knowledge delivers, but a more ruthless kind. He knew that such power, hoarded and turned to selfish and hurtful usage, destroys families, fellowship and, indeed, people.

So, Blake, in his writing and art, runs up against his own vulnerability, as child or adult: that of being at the mercy of worldly forces, manifested in individuals who have more muscle than spirit, more power than compassion. This knowledge infuses his poetry, nowhere more than in the final poem of *Songs of Experience*, "A Divine Image," beginning so famously:

Cruelty has a human heart,
And Jealousy a human face.

And ending:

The human dress is forged in iron,
The human form a fiery forge,

The human face a furnace seal'd,
The human heart a hungry gorge.

By the way, I love Blake's dropping of the word "is" in lines following the first, improving the meter and, dare I say, foretelling the sprung rhythm of Gerard Manley Hopkins?

More fundamentally, the poem is nearly too painful, too shot through with the awful realization of what dark forces can constitute the human heart and form. All this set out in such expression—alliteration at its very best, internal and end rhymes, and rhythm and meter of extraordinary art—yet none of this for its own sake, all for the profound task of heartfelt meaning.

Then there's also the contrast we see with the final poem in *Songs of Innocence*, "Little Boy Found," where God and the boy's mother shower the boy with love. This strikes me as an essential story of his time, our time; indeed, of the whole vast human endeavor.

Blake knew something profound: you must fear most not an angry God or a devil, but the human being next to you or down the street whose intentions are not peaceful.

Early on in your most recent, you write, "We want to know what we cannot know." Might this be a foundation sentiment of Romanticism? Wordsworth's sorrow too deep for tears; Keats's not knowing if what he's seen, the nightingale, is even real; Shelley's "if only" posture which yearns to sing so all would listen, yet cannot (only the skylark can do that). None grasp and hold what they would ultimately know; they live without that fulfillment.

But not so the classical mind. I'd posit that its alternative is, "I want to know what I *can* know." Greek tragedies, culminating with the Oedipus trilogy, take the quest for what is ultimately knowable to its endpoint. Oedipus puts all on the line to discover his lineage and what he's done in ignorance—killed his father and married his mother. In the end *he knows,* albeit that knowledge is so unbearable that he mutilates himself irrevocably. Remarkable that he doesn't kill himself; no, he chooses to live with the hard-won knowledge he'd sought and the attending guilt, that has destroyed his eyes.

On to the section where you provide us with a proposed title for this book (*Between Silence and Voice*), you've perhaps forged the

Most to be feared: the cruel intentions of the human heart

bridge between the Romantic and Classical: you've underscored the journey out of silence, to a final place in which to reside—voice. Any and all writers, no matter Hebrew, classical, romantic, modern, existential, nihilistic—all come to this very spot. Even for Job, for Beckett, for Primo Levi, one thing only is unacceptable: silence. To divert to Hamlet, yes, Shakespeare allows him to make silence his final condition, but not before he'd filled the stage with words.

As for Ken Kesey and his failed screenplay: I say "failed" with hesitation. To him it may have been a success, same as his novel. But not so to Hollywood, which had an entirely other agenda—to put audiences at ease with the film, and thus in movie-house seats. To achieve this, the studio bosses preferred Kesey's silence, in return for money. The result was an award-winning movie at the cost of Kesey's abiding hatred, echoing that of Holden Caulfield.

Now, my branch of commercial writing was advertising, but I went in at age 30 with no illusions about what I was doing: arriving at a marketplace with a skill to sell, knowing that my bosses would pay me well to shape that skill to their ends and to meet a public need.

Occasionally, people who knew that I also wrote poetry and prose (no plays yet) sometimes asked me, "Won't writing commercially kill your poetry?" I had already asked myself the same question. And my answer was, "If writing for money can do that, then my poetry—and my impulse to write it—must have been weak indeed, and of no account." That turned out to be not the case.

We may sometimes "sell our souls"—but thankfully the sale is not permanent

I think the real question was, did I sell my soul? My answer: yes, but only to buy it back again, night after night.

The Mailer anecdote is informative in this connection. My reaction is that working to find his authentic voice was not worth the struggle for him. That he preferred ventriloquism, a product of show business. Indeed, he was so good at it that it made him the quintessential showman, and brought him what he surely wanted: fame.

In Mailer's terms, then, does America reward the ventriloquist, the phony, more than the true authentic?

Whatever the answer, I sympathize with your view that Mailer was closer to his authentic self in his journalism.

I, like you, my very good friend, want to know. And as I wind down what has been a deeply satisfying set of conversations with you, I want to say that I love and respect the deep impulse in you to attend to the sounds of what is true, and reject the dissonance in what is false. I strive to be that way too. But I want to know what I *can* know.

It is the voice of Jake, an inmate I knew in my prison work, who had outgrown the awful crime of his youth and wanted only to tell his victim's loved ones that he grieves and seeks forgiveness, though they turn a deaf ear.

It's the now-stilled voice of Yaffa Weitzman, New York psychotherapist, who for eighteen years held my feet to the fire of my own authenticity.

The voice, finally, of Sharon Kuroki, who loves me and whom I love and in whose eyes I always see love's power.

These I can and do know.

David

# 33. "As If Dictated by Someone Just Outside the Room"

David,

For my final word, I return to Norman Mailer, who would have turned 100 years old in 2023, had he lived so long. I recently published a letter in *The New Yorker* in honor of those many years, mentioning that, in my view, he was not a Jewish boy from Brooklyn escaping his identity, but a generous talent and a true mensch. So, to celebrate his birthday, let me end our book with a quote from one of his—*Armies of the Night*.

**Reach for the next promise!** Speaking about the work of the literary writer, Mailer advises that we "reach for the next promise, which is usually hidden in some word or phrase just a shift to the side of one's conscious intent . . . as if dictated by someone just outside the room."

Bob

# Acknowledgments

By Robert Waxler

I have dedicated this book to my wife Linda and to my sons Jonathan and Jeremy. They are always with me, always providing the gift of inspiration. I also want to thank the early readers of this book, who offered many valuable insights and always encouraged me to carry on. They have been friends, worthy critics and exceptional colleagues for a long time. I am especially thankful to David Sarles, Carl Schinasi, Jim Marlow, Richard Larschan, Howard Senzel, Paul Bresnick, Jim Cronin, Jean Trounstine, Martha Pennington, Bob Kane, and Tom Dargan.

I am grateful to my brother David Waxler who offered much wisdom, especially on the Zohar and Jewish mysticism and to Robert Pontbriand who helped me develop a perspective on Greek philosophy and Jewish tradition.

I will never forget the thousands of students in my classes at UMass Dartmouth, their contributions to my love and understanding of literature and dialogue. Listening to them has given me a unique sense of joy and a deep commitment to the humanities. And the participants in the Changing Lives Through Literature program (the probationers, the judges, the probation officers, the facilitators) have also contributed much to this book with their intelligence and often surprising perspectives through conversations around the seminar tables.

I also owe thanks to Jo-Anne Cooley at the UMassD library and the entire library staff there, who were always willing to find a book I requested no matter where on earth it might be.

Special thanks to Karl Weber, our editor and publisher, a genuine partner in our efforts and a man no doubt dedicated to the making of books to help preserve our freedom and democracy. And Brian Singer, our cover designer, who, I believe, has captured the spirit of our intent.

Forever grateful to Dr. David Ryan, my oncologist and good friend, who has taught me more than I ever expected to know.

And, of course, David Beckman, my faithful amigo. If he had not shown up, this book would never have existed.

## By David Beckman

Early influences: my mother, who read to me as a child, combining language and love. My father, whose devotion to books and reading showed me what the life of the mind is. My older sister, Kathie, whose early achievements showed me what success looked like. Mrs. Paulson, high school English teacher, who saw and encouraged my writing spark.

College teachers: Professor Van Nostrand (American literature), Professor Bernstein (Shakespeare), and Professor Philbrick, who oversaw my senior thesis on poet Rupert Brooke.

In New York—commercial writing: Stan Winston, copy chief, Ogilvy and Mather advertising, who gave me my first job. Emily Soel, creative director, Rapp Collins advertising, who facilitated my growth. Roy Beauchamp, Time Inc., who ushered me into that hotbed of commercial writing. James B. Hayes, Discover Magazine publisher, who championed me. Jo Fox, designer extraordinaire and my creative partner for 15 years.

Also in New York—fiction and playwriting: Ann Loring, and all in her Friday night seminars, where I spread my wings. Novelist Hugh Nissenson, who took me seriously. Peter Cherisi, of Derrynane Books, my first publisher.

In California—poetry: Ed Coletti, Greg Randall, Dave Seter, Katherine Hastings, Jodi Hotel, and Toni Wilks, providing fertile ground where I grew (and grow yet) as a poet. Susan Terris and David St. John, who affirmed the result. Theater: Sixth Street Playhouse, which produced my first play, Russell Kaltschmidt, who directed it, and Lennie Dean, who encouraged me as actor and playwright.

Finally, Bob Waxler, college friend, fellow-poet and my partner in this book. Deep thanks, amigo.

# Index

# About the Authors

*The authors at Brown, 1966.*
*David Beckman (left), Robert Waxler (right).*

R OBERT P. WAXLER graduated with a B.A. from Brown University, an M.A. from Boston College, and a Ph.D. from Stony Brook University. He is a Professor Emeritus at University of Massachusetts Dartmouth, where he also served as Chairman of the English Department, Associate Dean of the College of Arts and Sciences, and Dean of Continuing Education and Summer Programs.

Professor Waxler is cofounder of the Center for Jewish Culture at UMass Dartmouth and served as the Center's codirector for fifteen years. He also cofounded Changing Lives Through Literature, an internationally celebrated alternative sentencing program for criminal offenders, which has continued its work for over thirty years.

Waxler has authored/co-authored several books, including *The Risk of Reading* (Bloomsbury), *Why Reading Books Still Matters* (Routledge), *Finding a Voice* (University of Michigan), *Losing Jonathan* (Spinner), *Changing Lives Through*

*Literature* (Notre Dame), *Transforming Literacy* (Brill), and *Courage to Walk* (Spinner).

He has also published numerous articles about literature, language and communication in a variety of scholarly journals, essay collections, magazines and newspapers. The author and his work have been featured in *Parade Magazine, Le Novel Observateur,* the *New York Times,* and on National Public Radio.

He lives with his wife Linda Lassoff Waxler, a retired math teacher, in Dartmouth, Massachusetts, where they have enjoyed married life together for fifty-six years.

Robert Waxler can be contacted at rwaxler@umassd.edu.


D AVID BECKMAN graduated cum laude with honors from Brown and holds a Diploma in English Studies from the University of Edinburgh, Scotland.

His poetry chapbooks include *Language Factory of the Mind* (Finishing Line Press), *Phantasia,* (mgv2/publishing, France), and *Times Three,* poems from New York and California. His poems have appeared in many anthologies, most recently in *America We Call Your Name* from Sixteen Rivers Press. He has been nominated twice for the Pushcart Poetry Prize.

His plays have been produced in New York, Santa Monica, Santa Cruz, Dallas and in a number of theaters in Northern California.

His prose includes *To Walk in Paris,* travel vignettes written with Sharon Kuroki Beckman (McCaa Books), and his novel *Under Pegasus* (Derrynane Press, New York.)

In his parallel life, David worked as a promotion writer in New York City from 1977 to 2003, in ad agencies and for Time Inc. He was a senior writer in Time's magazine group, then Promotion Director of *Discover* magazine.

David and his wife, Sharon, lived in New York for 35 years before they moved to Santa Rosa, California, in 2003. He currently volunteers for the World Affairs Council of Sonoma County, plays golf, disc golf, and billiards, and writes poetry and plays. He and his wife enjoy volunteer work, family, friends, reading, yoga, and travel.

# About the Cover Artist

B RIAN SINGER, also known as someguy, created the image on the cover of this book, titled *Geometry #28*. Singer is a practitioner of various forms of art, including his Edgework series, in which three-dimensional images are created by physically reassembling printed books. Singer has described the process this way:

> I start with old paperback books that have green, red or yellow edging. They are acquired through library sales and range from science fiction to mystery, spy thrillers, and romance novels. The books are then cut up and organized based on the edge color or pattern.

*Geometry* #28, with its glowing, mosaic-like pattern in shades of yellow, beige, brown, and red formed from cross-section pieces of old books, is a beautiful example of Singer's work.

"By deconstructing books and reassembling them," Singer has written, "I seek to breathe new life into millions of hidden words, sentences, and stories."

In a similar way, *You Say, I Say* assembles its two authors' personal reactions to a wide-ranging array of literary works—poems, plays, novels, and critical essays—into a new and vibrant pattern that reflects their lives, experiences, and insights, all in the context of a lifelong friendship. Thus, we believe that Brian Singer's artwork and the contents of this book make an effective pairing. We're grateful to Brian for granting us permission to adapt his work for this purpose.

Learn more about Brian Singer at www.someguy.is.

www.ingramcontent.com/pod-product-compliance
Lightning Source LLC
Chambersburg PA
CBHW021621120626
46545CB00001B/336